DESCRIPTIVE CATALOGING FOR THE AACR2R AND USMARC

A How-To-Do-It Workbook

LARRY MILLSAP
TERRY ELLEN FERL

*HOW-TO-DO-IT MANUALS
FOR LIBRARIES*
Number 15

Series Editor: Bill Katz

NEAL-SCHUMAN PUBLISHERS, INC.
New York, London

Published by Neal-Schuman Publishers, Inc.
100 Varick Street
New York, NY 10013

Copyright © 1991 by The Regents of the University of California

Printed and bound in the United. States of America

Library of Congress Cataloging-in-Publication Data

Millsap, Larry.
    Descriptive cataloging for the AACR2R and USMARC : a how-to-do-it
workbook / Larry Millsap, Terry Ellen Ferl.
        p.   cm. — (How-to-do-it manuals for libraries no. 15)
    Includes bibliographical references and index.
    ISBN 1-55570-098-5
    1. Anglo-American cataloguing rules—Problems, exercises, etc.
2. MARC System—United States—Problems, exercises, etc.
3. Descriptive cataloging—Problems, exercises, etc. I. Ferl,
Terry Ellen. II. Title. III. Series.
Z694.15.A56M55   1991
025.3′2—dc20   91-31139
                                                        CIP

CONTENTS

FOREWORD

The University Library of the University of California, Santa Cruz has been making machine-readable cataloging records since the campus was opened in 1965, well before national MARC standards were accepted. We have learned a great deal about the importance of making standard records, transportable from one automated system to another, as we worked to revise these early non-standard records. As a member of MOBAC, the Monterey Bay Cooperative Library System, the library was very pleased to be able to share our hard-earned knowledge with the other libraries in this multi-type consortium.

This workbook grew out of a series of workshops that UCSC catalogers presented for MOBAC. MOBAC is planning to use the workbook for training of new catalogers. It is our hope that other libraries making the switch to machine-readable cataloging will also find this workbook helpful to their cataloging staff.

Allan J. Dyson
University Librarian
UC Santa Cruz

PREFACE

This workbook is designed to give catalogers practice in creating original descriptive cataloging records which can be shared with other libraries in an automated environment. It is especially intended for catalogers in small libraries who have neither a great deal of experience making MARC records in many different formats nor more experienced colleagues nearby who can provide advice.

We assume that the reader is acquainted with the *Anglo-American Cataloguing Rules,* but may profit from structured practice. Bibliographic information is presented in a series of exercises which require application of cataloging rules and machine-readable coding conventions common to the cataloging community. The exercises consist of title page and/or other information which the reader will use to create a cataloging record on a workform. Following each workform is the completed catalog record (or "answer") and an explanation citing the rules which have been applied. We have tried to include among the examples materials for which copy is unlikely to be available on the cataloging utilities, e.g., unpublished items.

The assignment of subject headings and the application of classification schedules are not covered in this workbook.

The essential tools for creating original descriptive cataloging records in machine-readable form are the *Anglo-American Cataloguing Rules,* 2nd ed., 1988 Revision *(AACR2R),* and the *USMARC Format for Bibliographic Data.* The MARC format will be familiar to catalogers who have used a major bibliographic utility such as the OCLC Online System, or any of a variety of MARC format implementations such as *Bibliofile.* Because of their importance in the cataloging community, the *Library of Congress Rule Interpretations,* or *LCRIs,* have also become a basic tool for original cataloging based on *AACR2R.*

The reader must have access to manuals for some version of USMARC, in order to prepare cataloging records for entry in a computerized data base. Availability of the *LCRIs* is also essential for the completion of the exercises. To complete the exercises for archives and manuscripts, the reader will need to consult Steven L. Hensen's *Archives, personal papers, and manuscripts* (2nd ed., 1989).

1 THE RULES

DESCRIPTION

The *Anglo-American Cataloguing Rules,* 2nd ed., 1988 revision, is the current descriptive cataloging code. Part I (Chapters 1-13) provides for describing an item in terms of its title, publisher, physical characteristics, etc. Part II (Chapters 21-25) deals with the choice and form of headings (access points) by which the description is presented to users of the catalog.

The most essential chapter of *AACR2R* is Chapter 1, which contains the general rules for description. Subsequent chapters in part I frequently refer back to this chapter rather than repeat its provisions. Chapter 2 contains the rules for describing books. Chapters 3-11 give the rules for describing non-book materials, and Chapter 12 provides for description of serials. Chapter 13 gives the rules for preparing analytic records for a part or parts of an item that is described elsewhere in a more comprehensive record, should a cataloging agency which to do so. If an item falls into more than one category (such as serially-issued maps), more than one chapter must be consulted.

CHOOSING ACCESS POINTS

Part II of *AACR2R* applies to all library materials, regardless of the medium. Chapter 21 tells how to choose the main entry and when to add other access points to a record. Chapters 22-24 explain how to establish the headings for personal, geographic, and corporate names, so that the forms of the names will be consistent throughout the catalog. Chapter 25, on uniform titles, deals with the problem of providing a consistent entry in the catalog for a work that has appeared in different editions, translations, etc. (e.g., the *Bible,* Shakespeare's *Hamlet,* Beethoven's *Ninth Symphony*).

CHOOSING MAIN ENTRY

Ultimately, there is no substitute for consulting the specific rules when creating original cataloging records in a shared data base.

However, the principles for *choice of main entry* in Chapter 21 may be summarized fairly briefly.

When there is a single personal author chiefly responsible for the creation of the intellectual or artistic content of a work, the heading for that person is the main entry for the work. When there are two or three persons with more or less equal responsibility as author, the heading for the first named is the main entry. If there is no one identified as author, or there are more than three personal authors identified, the title of the work is chosen for the main entry.

When a work emanates from a corporate body, the body is the main entry only if the criteria in 21.1B2 are met. Corporate authorship is quite restricted in *AACR2R*. The *LCRIs* for Rule 21.1B2 are helpful in interpreting the rather brief statements of the conditions under which a corporate body is chosen as the main entry for a work.

There are also many situations of mixed responsibility that affect choice of main entry, such as those in which one person has modified, adapted, or performed the work of another, or where an artist and author collaborate on a work. The very significant factor in cases of mixed responsibility is how the chief source of information presents the item being cataloged. Two people can perform identical functions in the production of a work, but, if the title page identifies one as an author and the other as editor, the first will be a main entry but the second will not. Non-book materials (for example, maps, computer files, and motion pictures) may pose special problems in choice of main entry because of the *AACR2R* definition of authorship.

FORM OF ACCESS POINTS

Once the cataloger has decided which access points to add to the description of an item, the *form* of these access points must be determined. For most North American libraries, the forms established by the Library of Congress are the authoritative forms. When, however, a name has not yet been established in the LC Name Authority File, the cataloger must consult *AACR2R* Chapters 22-24 (and Chapter 25, if appropriate) to establish the form of the name (or uniform title) to be used in a record.

The general rule for choosing a name in order to make a heading for a person is deceptively simple: choose the name by which he or she is commonly known. The cataloger may sometimes have to choose among different names when the author uses pseudonyms or has changed his or her name. Also, the same name may appear in different forms. The form may vary either in fullness or, for names in nonroman script, transliteration. An example of the latter case is Muammar Qaddafi; there are 29 references for the various forms of that name in the LC Name Authorities.

Once the cataloger has chosen the name to be used, there are additional rules for forming the heading. The entry element, that part of the name under which the person would normally be listed in authoritative alphabetic lists in his or her language, must be determined. Titles of nobility or royal status must be added to the headings for some names. Dates of birth and death and spelled out forms of names represented by initials are routinely added to name headings by LC catalogers when they are available.

Geographic names must be established for use in the headings for governments and non-governmental entities. They are also needed to distinguish corporate bodies with the same name, and as additions to corporate names, such as conference names. The general rule in Chapter 23 is to use the English form of a place name, if there is one in general use. Again, the LC Name Authority File provides the authoritative forms for geographic names. The Library of Congress determines these forms from gazetteers and other reference sources published in English-speaking countries. When these sources do not yield a form, the vernacular form is chosen. Dealing with changes of place names and providing consistent additions to place names are examples of complexities associated with establishing geographic names.

The general rule in Chapter 24, "Headings for Corporate Bodies," is to enter a corporate body directly under the name by which it is commonly identified. This name is determined from items issued by the body in its language, or, failing that, from reference sources. Problems in establishing a corporate body's name may arise if, for example, the body changes its name, if two different bodies have identical names, and whenever a decision must be made as to whether or not a body should be entered subordinately to another body. Also, there are special rules of entry for names of government bodies and officials, legislative bodies, courts, armed forces, embassies, religious bodies and officials, etc. Consulting the *LCRIs* is essential to establishing a name exactly as the Library of Congress would establish it, should you be the first cataloger to contribute a name heading to a shared data base.

RULE INTERPRETATIONS

AACR2R leaves a number of areas open for local interpretation, local option, and an individual cataloger's judgment. In the interest of achieving a national standard for the presentation of bibliographic data in cataloging records, the major bibliographic utilities and cataloging agencies have endorsed the rule interpretations of the Library of Congress. The answers to the exercises in this workbook incorporate the *LCRIs* whenever appropriate.*

---

* Ben R. Tucker, Chief of the Library of Congress Office for Descriptive Cataloging Policy, provides an interesting account of the development of the rule interpretations at LC in "Ask Me No Questions and I'll Write You No RIs" (*The Conceptual Foundations of Descriptive Cataloging*. San Diego: Academic Press, © 1989).

2 MARC FORMAT

In the late 1960s, the Library of Congress developed the MARC (*MA*chine *R*eadable *C*ataloging) format for communication of bibliographic information. A MARC-based record identifies data for computer recognition and manipulation, permitting the exchange and sharing of the record across automated systems.

The current *USMARC Format for Bibliographic Data* provides for bibliographic records in seven different specifications: books, archival and manuscript control, computer files, maps, music, visual materials, and serials. In most implementations of USMARC, these materials are cataloged in individual formats: the cataloger "calls up" a workform for data entry containing tags and coding appropriate to whichever type of material is being cataloged. (In some implementations of MARC, for example OCLC's, music is divided into separate formats for music scores and sound recordings.)

DEFINITIONS

The following definitions of USMARC components should be helpful to catalogers.

Record: the collection of fields containing machine-readable information about a separately cataloged item. Each record is made up of control fields and bibliographic data fields.

Field: data in a record that forms a logical unit.

Variable fields: There are two kinds. The more familiar are the *variable data fields*. These are of varying length and carry information such as the main entry heading, title, call number, ISBN, notes, and added entries for a work. This is the information that is displayed to catalog users. Each variable field of this type is identified by a three-digit code called a *tag,* followed by two character positions reserved for *indicators*. The tags are in the range 0XX-8XX. Indicators are used, for example, to represent the number of characters ignored in filing or sorting fields, and to signify text that is to be supplied in a catalog display, like the word "Contents:" at the beginning of a contents note.

The less familiar kind of variable field is the *variable control field*. These fields, which are tagged 00X, contain neither indicator positions nor subfield codes. They are structurally different from the variable data fields. They may contain either a single data element or a series of fixed-length data elements identified by relative character position. For example, the *007 Physical Description Fixed Field* is used to code physical characteristics of an item, such as color (of a map), dimensions (of a motion picture film), speed (of a sound recording), etc. The *008 Fixed-Length Data Elements Field* contains 40 character positions for coding information about the record as a whole and about special bibliographic aspects of the item being cataloged. Examples of such information are: the date a record was entered in the data base, the publication date of an item, the nature of the contents of an item, the frequency of publication of an item, whether or not it is a government publication, etc. The coded information in these fields is, of course, not displayed to the catalog user, but it allows libraries to take advantage of a computer's capabilities to manipulate data in ways that enhance retrieval. For instance, limiting retrievals by language and date are common methods of refining a search in online catalogs. The computer gets the information needed to do this from the data in the variable control fields.

The Leader: This field is fixed in length at 24 character positions, It is the first field of a USMARC record, and it provides information for the processing of the record. Included are numbers or coded values for information such as record length, type of record (e.g., music, map, etc.), and descriptive cataloging form (e.g., Non-ISBD; AACR2, etc.). This data may also be useful to the enhancement of retrieval.

The Directory: This part of the record is an index to the location of the variable fields within a record. This information is not visible to the inputting cataloger or the catalog user.

Subfields: Within each field, information may be subdivided into smaller logical units. Each smaller unit is called a subfield. Example: a typical imprint contains three subfields: Place, publisher, and date. Each subfield is identified by a character called a subfield code. The code is usually a lowercase letter and is preceded by a delimiter. In OCLC, the delimiter is a double dagger. In LC documents, the $ is used as the delimiter.

Content Designators: Because tags, indicators and subfield codes identify each element of information that may occur in a bibliographic record, they are known collectively as content designators.

IMPLEMENTATIONS OF USMARC

In order to make it easier to enter and edit data in the leader and the control fields, the bibliographic utilities have developed screen displays that separate the various elements. In OCLC, parts of the leader and the 008 are combined in an arbitrary order in the fixed field. Each element is identified by a mnemonic tag. In OCLC, elements of the 007 are separated by OCLC-defined subfields. In a Bibliofile workform, the leader is presented as a string and each element of the 008 is identified by a mnemonic tag. The order of elements in that display follows the order of appearance in the 008. In the exercises and workforms, we have used the kind of display found in Bibliofile.

When a cataloger requests a workform, the system supplies certain elements. It supplies record status, type, and bibliographic level (position 05-07) in the leader and date entered (position 00-05) in the 008. In our examples of completed records, we have also entered *a* in position 18 of the leader to indicate that *AACR2* was the cataloging code used to prepare the records. Since the 007 is a relatively brief field, we have presented it just as a string.

Following is an example of the leader and 008 data in the USMARC format, in an OCLC record, and in a Bibliofile record. A scale is supplied below the data in the USMARC format in order to show the position of data.

FORMAT INTEGRATION

After 1993, several significant changes may be implemented in the USMARC format. These changes are part of an effort which began in the early 1980s to bring together in one publication the separate format documents for books, serials, etc., and the updates that are issued periodically. In 1987, an integrated edition that accomplished this, *USMARC format for bibliographic data including guidelines for content designation,* was published.

Subsequent format integration work will result in coded values being assignable to any types of materials for which they are appropriate. For example, the *seriality* of nonprint materials will be able to be represented. This has not been possible in the past because the serials specification does not allow inclusion of certain characteristics of nonprint materials, and the specifications for

---

Leader and 008 data in three formats.

USMARC

```
Leader          nam          a
008     900701s1987    nyua       b     00110 eng d
posi    0000000000011111111112222222222233333333333
tion:   01234567890123456789012345678901234567890123456789
```

OCLC

```
OCLC: 13456478        Rec stat: n  Entrd: 900701
Type: a Bibl lvl: m Govt pub:    Lang: eng Source: d Illus: a
Repr:     Enc lvl:     Conf pub: 0 Ctry: nyu Date tp: s M/F/B: 10
Indx: 1 Mod rec:      Festschr: 0 Cont: b
Desc: a Int lvl:      Dates: 1987,
```

Bibliofile

```
Leader              nam          a
Fixed Data 008
  Entrd: 900701  Dat tp: s Dates: 1987,      Ctry: nyu Illus: a
  Int lvl:    Repr:    Cont: b   Govt pub:    Conf pub: 0 Festsch: 0
  Indx: 1 M/E: 1 Fict: 0 Bio:    Lang: eng Mod rec:     Source: d
```

---

nonprint materials do not consistently accommodate serial characteristics.

To prepare for this new flexibility in USMARC, some elements will be made obsolete, some will be extended to make them valid in each of the seven basic forms of materials, and some elements will be deleted altogether. A few completely new elements will be added. Because bibliographic records now circulate among a great number of systems (e.g., bibliographic utilities, vendors, the Library of Congress), considerable lead-time and careful coordination of these USMARC changes is necessary.*

---

* The evolution of format integration is described by Walt Crawford in *MARC for Library Use*. 2nd. ed. Boston: G. K. Hall, 1989 (pp. 221-241).

3 EXERCISES

This section contains 46 exercises for the reader to complete in each of the seven USMARC specification types: books, archival and manuscripts control, computer files, maps, music, visual materials, and serials.

Each exercise consists of four pages. The first page contains title and other information to be used in completing the blank workform on the facing page. The third page gives an explanation of the rules used to complete the cataloging record printed on the fourth page.

In the introduction to *AACR2R* (0.29), general guidance is given for choosing the level of description, or amount of detail. The three recommended levels are then presented in Rule 1.0D. The records in this workbook have been completed generally at the second level of description.

Appropriate values have been supplied in the leader on the workforms, as described on page 6 of this workbook. For serials, however, the value for leader position 19, which indicates the need for a related record, should be supplied by the cataloger as appropriate.

According to USMARC, supplying data elements in the 008 field is mandatory if applicable in some cases and optional in others. In the completed exercises, values have been supplied for each 008 element whenever the information is evident from the description.

Beginning on page 191 are 46 review questions to test the reader's ability to identify the correct rule in various cataloging situations. Answers to these questions are given on pages 196-200.

BOOKS

The special rules for description of books are in Chapter 2 of AACR2. Chapters 21 through 25 are used for choosing entries and forming headings.

Example 1

TITLE PAGE

WEEDS

an illustrated botanical guide to the weeds of Australia

B.A. Auld and R.W. Medd

with original line drawings by
Julie M. Morris

Agricultural Research and Veterinary Centre, Orange
Department of Agriculture New South Wales

Inkata Press
Melbourne   Sydney

OTHER INFORMATION

There are viii and 255 pages with illustrations, some in color. From the verso: first published 1987; ISBN 0 909605 37 8. There is an index and a bibliography on page 239. The book is 26.3 cm tall.

BOOKS WORKFORM

Leader   nam   a
Fixed Data 008
  Entrd: nnnnnn Dat tp: Dates: Ctry: Illus:
  Int lvl: Repr: Cont: Govt pub: Conf pub: Festsch:
  Indx: M/E: Fict: Bio: Lang: Mod rec: Source:

020

041 _

1__ _ _

245 _ _

250

260 _

300

4__ _ _

5__

7__ _ _

7__ _ _

8__ _ _

Choice of entry: Responsibility for this work is shared by two authors and an illustrator. Rule 21.11A1 says the entry should be under the heading appropriate for the text. 21.6C1 says to enter under the first of two authors when principal responsibility is not attributed to one of them. The rule also provides for an added entry for the second author. Choice of name and form of headings is determined by 22.1A, 22.5, and the options in 22.17 and 22.18. An added entry is made for the illustrator only if the criteria in 21.30K2 are met. The criteria aren't met here.

Description: The title and statement of responsibility are transcribed according to 2.1B1, 2.1E1, and 2.1F1.

The publication data is transcribed according to 1.4C5, 2.4D1, and 2.4F1.

The physical description is given according to 2.5B2, 2.5C1, 2.5C3, and 2.5D1.

The bibliography and index notes are transcribed according to the LCRI for 2.7B18.

The standard book number is included in the record following 2.8B1. However, it is included in field 020 as a string without spacing or punctuation, not in the way the rule directs.

Leader   nam   a
Fixed Data 008
  Entrd: nnnnnn Dat tp: s Dates: 1987,   Ctry: at Illus: a
  Int lvl: Repr: Cont: b Govt pub: Conf pub: 0 Festsch: 0
  Indx: 1 M/E: 1 Fict: 0 Bio: Lang: eng Mod rec: Source: d

020   0909605378

100 10 Auld, B. A. $q (Bruce Archibald), $d 1945-

245 10 Weeds : $b an illustrated botanical guide to the weeds of Australia / $c B.A. Auld and R.W. Medd ; with original line drawings by Julie M. Morris.

260 0   Melbourne : $b Inkata Press, $c 1987.

300   viii, 255 p. : $b ill. (some col.) ; $c 27 cm.

504   Includes bibliographical references (p. 239)

500   Includes index.

700 10 Medd, R. W. $q (Richard William), $d 1946-

Example 2

TITLE PAGE

Approaches to Social Research

Royce Singleton, Jr.
Holy Cross College

Bruce C. Straits and Margaret M. Straits
University of California, Santa Barbara

Ronald J. McAllister
Northeastern University

New York   Oxford
OXFORD UNIVERSITY PRESS
1988

OTHER INFORMATION

The ISBN is 0-19-504469-X; there are xviii and 541 pages including graphs, tables, and diagrams. The book is 24.6 cm tall. There is a bibliography on pages 497 to 515, and there is an index.

BOOKS WORKFORM

Leader   nam   a
Fixed Data 008
  Entrd: nnnnnn Dat tp: Dates: Ctry: Illus:
  Int lvl: Repr: Cont: Govt pub: Conf pub: Festsch:
  Indx: M/E: Fict: Bio: Lang: Mod rec: Source:

020

041 _

1_ _ _

245 _ _

250

260 _

300

4_ _ _

5_

7_ _ _

7_ _ _

8_ _ _

Choice of entry: This is a work of shared responsibility. There are four authors and none is given principal responsibility. Therefore entry is under title following 21.6C2, and Singleton receives an added entry. The form of heading follows 22.1, 22.4, and 22.5. If it were necessary to distinguish Singleton from his father in the catalog and no dates were available, 22.19B1 provides for the inclusion of *Jr.* in the heading. Otherwise it is not included.

Description: The title is transcribed according to 2.1B1. Only the first named author is transcribed in the statement of responsibility according to 1.1F5. The title *Jr.* is transcribed according to 1.1F7c since it is necessary to identify the author.

Only New York is transcribed in the publication information following 1.4C5. The publisher and date are transcribed following 2.4D1 and 2.4F1.

Physical description is given according to 2.5B2, 2.5C1, and 2.5D1. 2.5C2 has not been applied because LCRI says to use *ill.* to cover all forms of illustration.

The notes have been included according to the LCRI for 2.7B18.

The standard book number is included in the record following 2.8B1. However, it is included in field 020 as a string without spacing or punctuation, not in the way the rule directs.

Leader   nam   a
Fixed Data 008
 Entrd: nnnnnn Dat tp: s Dates: 1988,   Ctry: nyu Illus: a
 Int lvl: Repr: Cont: b Govt pub: Conf pub: 0 Festsch: 0
 Indx: 1 M/E: 0 Fict: 0 Bio: Lang: eng Mod rec: Source: d

020   019504469X

245 00 Approaches to social research / $c Royce Singleton, Jr. ... [et al.].

260 0 New York : $b Oxford University Press, $c 1988.

300   xviii, 541 p. : $b ill. ; $c 25 cm.

504   Includes bibliographical references (p. 497-515)

500   Includes index.

700 10 Singleton, Royce.

Example 3

TITLE PAGE

Paul Gauguin

Letters to his Wife and Friends

Edited by Maurice Malingue
Translated by Henry J. Stenning

The World Publishing Company
Cleveland and New York

OTHER INFORMATION

The pages are numbered xix, then [20] to 255. There are 16 leaves of illustration not included in the page numbering. The book is 21.3 cm tall. On verso of the title page: published April 1949.

BOOKS WORKFORM

Leader   nam   a
Fixed Data 008
  Entrd: nnnnnn Dat tp: Dates: Ctry: Illus:
  Int lvl: Repr: Cont: Govt pub: Conf pub: Festsch:
  Indx: M/E: Fict: Bio: Lang: Mod rec: Source:

020

041 _

1__ __ __

245 __ __

250

260 _

300

4__ __ __

5__

7__ __ __

7__ __ __

8__ __ __

Choice of entry: This is a work of mixed responsibility. The letters, not the commentary, are emphasized and the biographer/critic is represented on the title page as the editor; so following 21.15B, Gauguin is the main entry. 21.14A says to enter a translation under the heading appropriate to the original. Choice of name and form of heading are determined by 22.1, 22.4, and 22.17. The editor is given an added entry according to 21.30D1. The translator does not meet the criteria set forth in 21.30K1 and so is not given an added entry.

Description: Following 1.1B2 *Paul Gauguin* is transcribed as the title proper because it is connected grammatically to the other title information by the word *his*. Other title information is transcribed following 2.1E1. Gauguin is not repeated in the statement of responsibility following 1.1F13. The rest of the statement of responsibility is transcribed following 2.1F1.

The first named place of publication, *Cleveland*, is transcribed following 1.4C5. Publisher and date follow 2.4D1 and 2.4F1. *Publishing* and *Company* are abbreviated according to Appendix B.9.

Physical description follows 2.5B2, 2.5B10 (for leaves of plates), 2.5C1, and 2.5D1 apply. Since the numbering changes from roman to arabic but continues the same sequence, the first part is ignored following 2.5B5.

Leader   nam   a
Fixed Data 008
  Entrd: nnnnnn Dat tp: s Dates: 1949,   Ctry: ohu Illus: a
  Int lvl: Repr: Cont: Govt pub: Conf pub: 0 Festsch: 0
  Indx: 0 M/E: 1 Fict: 0 Bio: d Lang: eng Mod rec: Source: d

041 1   eng $h fre

100 10 Gauguin, Paul, $d 1848-1903.

245 10 Paul Gauguin : $b letters to his wife and friends / $c edited by Maurice Malingue ; translated by Henry J. Stenning.

260 0   Cleveland : $b World Pub. Co., $c 1949.

300   255 p., [16] leaves of plates : $b ill. ; $c 22 cm.

700 10 Malingue, Maurice, $d 1903-

Example 4

TITLE PAGE

ROBERT FERNIER

GUSTAVE COURBET

with an Introduction by

RENE HUYGHE

FREDERICK A. PRAEGER
Publishers
New York   Washington

OTHER INFORMATION

The verso of the title page includes the following information:

Translated from the French by Marcus Bullock
Published in the United States of America in 1969
by Frederick A. Praeger, Inc., Publishers
© 1969 by "Silvana" Editoriale d'Arte, Milan
© English translation 1969 by Pall Mall Press, London
Library of Congress Catalog Card Number: 70-84856
Printed in Italy

There are 139 pages and the book is 28 cm. high; there are illustrations; some are in color. There is a bibliography on page 135, and there is an index.

BOOKS WORKFORM

Leader   nam   a
Fixed Data 008
  Entrd: nnnnnn Dat tp: Dates: Ctry: Illus:
  Int lvl: Repr: Cont: Govt pub: Conf pub: Festsch:
  Indx: M/E: Fict: Bio: Lang: Mod rec: Source:

020

041 _

1__ _ _

245 _ _

250

260 _

300

4__ _ _

5__

7__ _ _

7__ _ _

8__ _ _

Choice of entry: The book contains reproductions of the artist's work and text about the artist; the author of the text is represented as author on the title page and is the main entry in accordance with 21.17B. This rule prescribes an added entry for the artist. The choice of name and form of heading are determined by 22.1A and 22.5A1. The translator does not meet the criteria in 21.30K1 for an added entry.

Description: The title proper is transcribed according to 2.1B1. The is no other title information.

The statement of responsibility is transcribed according to 2.1F1.

There are two places listed where the publisher has offices; only the first is transcribed in accordance with 1.4C5. Of the publisher's name, only Praeger is transcribed in accordance with 1.4D2. The date is transcribed according to 2.4F1; the copyright date is not included since it is the same as the date of publication.

The physical description is given following 2.5B2, 2.5C3, and 2.5D1.

The bibliography note is included in the form prescribed by the LCRI for 2.7B18.

Leader   nam   a
Fixed Data 008
  Entrd: nnnnnn Dat tp: s Dates: 1969,   Ctry: nyu Illus: a
  Int lvl: Repr: Cont: b Govt pub: Conf pub: 0 Festsch: 0
  Indx: 1 M/E: 1 Fict: 0 Bio: b Lang: eng Mod rec: Source: d

010   70-84856

041 1   eng $h fre

100 10 Fernier, Robert.

245 10 Gustave Courbet / $c Robert Fernier ; with an introduction by
Rene Huyghe ; [translated from the French by Marcus Bullock].

260 0   New York : $b Praeger, $c 1969.

300   139 p. : $b ill. (some col.) ; $c 28 cm.

504   Includes bibliographical references (p. 135)

500   Includes index.

700 10 Courbet, Gustave, $d 1819-1877.

Example 5

TITLE PAGE

Emilio Carranza Castellanos

CUANDO

LOS RUSOS

invadieron

America del Norte

TRADICION. MEXICO. 1983

OTHER INFORMATION

The verso of the title page includes the following information:

Primera edicion:
Agosto de 1983.--1,500 ejemplares.

There are 123 pages with illustrations and some maps; the size is 21 cm. There is a bibliography on pages [117]-121.

BOOKS WORKFORM

Leader   nam   a
Fixed Data 008
  Entrd: nnnnnn Dat tp: Dates: Ctry: Illus:
  Int lvl: Repr: Cont: Govt pub: Conf pub: Festsch:
  Indx: M/E: Fict: Bio: Lang: Mod rec: Source:

020

041 _

1__ _ _

245 _ _

250

260 _

300

4__ _ _

5__

7__ _ _

7__ _ _

8__ _ _

Choice of entry: This is a work by a single personal author, and choice of entry is determined by 21.4A1. Form of heading is determined by 22.1A. The name contains a compound Spanish surname, so 22.5C4 is used to determine the entry element.

Description: The title is transcribed according to 2.1B1. The statement of responsibility is transposed to the required position per 1.1F3.

The edition statement is transcribed according to 2.2B1, Appendix C.3B1a, the LCRI for Appendix C.8B, and Appendix B.9. If the statement were instead, for example, "Seconda edicion, Agosto de 1983.—1,500 ejemplares," the cataloger would need to determine whether the item is "a copy of an earlier manifestation or an edition separate from the earlier manifestation needing its own bibliographic record" (LCRI for *AACR2R* 1.0). The input standards for the OCLC system say that "edition statements appearing on some foreign language publications (e.g., Romance language imprints) reflect printing information rather than edition information. If the edition statement appears in conjunction with the printer's name or the number of copies printed, generally consider the edition statement to reflect printing information and use the existing record [in OCLC]. In all other cases, use judgment. *If in doubt, use the existing record.*"

Publication information is transcribed according to 2.4C1, 2.4D1, and 2.4F1; and the physical description according to 2.5B2, the LCRI for 2.5C2, and 2.5D1.

The bibliography note is transcribed following the LCRI for 2.7B18.

Leader   nam   a
Fixed Data 008
  Entrd: nnnnnn Dat tp: s Dates: 1983   Ctry: mx Illus: ab
  Int lvl: Repr: Cont: b Govt pub: Conf pub: 0 Festsch: 0
  Indx: 0 M/E: 1 Fict: 0 Bio: Lang: spa Mod rec: Source: d

100 20 Carranza Castellanos, Emilio, $d 1931-

245 10 Cuando los rusos invadieron America del Norte / $c
Emilio Carranza Castellanos.

250   1. ed.

260 0   Mexico : $b Tradicion, $c 1983.

300   123 p. : $b ill., maps ; $c 21 cm.

504   Includes bibliographical references (p. [117]-121)

Example 6

TITLE PAGE

Proceedings of The Fourth Annual Eastern Regional Ground Water Conference

July 14-16, 1987
Radisson Hotel
Burlington, Vermont

Co-sponsored by

Association of Ground Water Scientists and Engineers (division of NWWA)
Environment Canada
Maine Department of Environmental Protection
Maine Geological Survey, Department of Conservation
Massachusetts Department of Environmental Quality Engineering
New England Interstate Water Pollution Control Commission
Petroleum Association for Conservation of the Canadian Environment
Association Petroliere pour la Conservation de l'Environment Canadien
Vermont Department of Water Resources and Environmental Engineering

Published by
National Water Well Association
6375 Riverside Dr.
Dublin, OH 43017

Produced by
Water Well Journal Publishing Co.
6375 Riverside Dr.
Dublin, OH 43017

OTHER INFORMATION

There are 783 pages; the book is 27.3 cm tall. There are illustrations and bibliographies. There is neither a copyright nor a publication date given.

BOOKS WORKFORM

Leader   nam   a
Fixed Data 008
  Entrd: nnnnnn Dat tp: Dates: Ctry: Illus:
  Int lvl: Repr: Cont: Govt pub: Conf pub: Festsch:
  Indx: M/E: Fict: Bio: Lang: Mod rec: Source:

020

041 _

1__ _ _

245 __ _ _

250

260 _

300

4__ _ _

5__

7__ _ _

7__ _ _

8__ _ _

Choice of entry: This book is the proceedings of a conference which is named prominently in the publication; so it meets the criterion of rule 21.1B2d for entry under the heading for the conference. The rules for choice and form of heading are 24.1A, 24.7. Rule 24.7A1 says to omit the indication of number and frequency from the name; 24.7B tells how to add the number, the date, and the place of the meeting in a formalized way.

The added entry for the corporate body is made according to 21.30D1.

Description: Title and statement of responsibility are transcribed according to 2.1B1, 2.1E1, and 2.1F1. Only the first of the co-sponsors is transcribed according to 1.1F5.

The publication information is transcribed according to 2.4.A1, 2.4C1, and 2.4F1. There is an option for also including the name of the printer, but it is not used.

The physical description is given according to 2.5B2, 2.5C1, and 2.5D1.

The bibliography note is transcribed according to the LCRI for 2.7B18.

Leader   nam   a
Fixed Data 008
 Entrd: nnnnnn Dat tp: s Dates: 1987,   Ctry: ohu Illus: a
 Int lvl: Repr: Cont: b Govt pub: Conf pub: 1 Festsch: 0
 Indx: 0 M/E: 1 Fict: 0 Bio: Lang: eng Mod rec: Source: d

111 20 Eastern Regional Ground Water Conference $n (4th : $d 1987 : $c Burlington, Vt.)

245 14 Proceedings of the fourth annual Eastern Regional Ground Water Conference : $b July 14-16, 1987, Radisson Hotel, Burlington, Vermont / $c co-sponsored by Association of Ground Water Scientists and Engineers (division of NWWA) ... [et al.].

260   Dublin, OH : $b National Water Well Association, $c [1987]

300   783 p. : $b ill. ; $c 28 cm.

504   Includes bibliographies.

710 20 Association of Ground Water Scientists and Engineers.

Example 7

TITLE PAGE

Asimov's Annotated

GILBERT & SULLIVAN

Text by William Schwenck Gilbert
Notes by Isaac Asimov

Doubleday
New York
1988

OTHER INFORMATION

On verso of title page: First edition. ISBN 0-38-52391-7

There are xiv and 1056 pages; the book is 26.7 cm tall. There are illustrations, bibliographical references on p. xiii, and an index. The book consists of the librettos of the Gilbert and Sullivan operettas with extensive notes by Asimov.

BOOKS WORKFORM

Leader   nam   a
Fixed Data 008
  Entrd: nnnnnn   Dat tp: Dates: Ctry: Illus:
  Int lvl: Repr: Cont: Govt pub: Conf pub: Festsch:
  Indx: M/E: Fict: Bio: Lang: Mod rec: Source:

020

041 _

1_ _ _ _

245 _ _ _

250

260 _

300

4_ _ _ _

5_ _

7_ _ _ _

7_ _ _ _

8_ _ _ _

Choice of entry: In determining main entry, the first choice is between Asimov and the heading for the original work. Rule 21.13C1 determines that the appropriate choice is the latter. Choosing the heading for the original work leads to an example of using an alternate rule. Rule 21.28A1 applies to this work. If that rule were followed, Gilbert, the librettist, would be the main entry. LCRI says to use the alternate rule; so the composer, Sullivan, is the main entry instead. The choice of name and form of heading are established according to 22.1A, 22.5A, 22.12B1 (which provides for the inclusion of the British term of honour), and 22.17.

The uniform title is established according to the special rules for music: 25.34C2, 25.35E1, and 25.34C3.

Gilbert is given an added entry according to the alternate rule for 21.28A and Asimov, according to 21.13C1.

Description: The title and statement of responsibility are transcribed according to 2.1B1 and 2.1F1; publication information, according to 2.4C1, 2.4D1, and 2.4F1; and physical description, according to 2.5B2, 2.5C1, and 2.5D1.

The edition information is presented in the form authorized in appendices B.9 and C.8A.

The bibliography and index notes are transcribed following the LCRI for 2.7B18.

The standard book number is included in the record following 2.8B1. However, it is included in field 020 as a string without spacing or punctuation, not in the way the rule directs.

Title added entries are made in accordance with 21.30J1.

Leader   nam   a
Fixed Data 008
  Entrd: nnnnnn Dat tp: s Dates: 1988,   Ctry: nyu Illus: a
  Int lvl: Repr: Cont: b Govt pub: Conf pub: 0 Festsch: 0
  Indx: 1 M/E: 1 Fict: 0 Bio: Lang: eng Mod rec: Source: d

020   0385239157

100 10 Sullivan, Arthur, $c Sir, $d 1842-1900.

240 10 Operas. $s Librettos. $k Selections

245 10 Asimov's annotated Gilbert & Sullivan / $c text by William Schwenck
Gilbert ; notes by Isaac Asimov.

250   1st ed.

260 0   New York : $b Doubleday, $c 1988.

300   xiv, 1056 p. : $b ill. ; $c 27 cm.

504   Includes bibliographical references (p. xiii)

500   Includes index.

700 10 Gilbert, W. S. $q (William Schwench), $d 1836-1911.

700 10 Asimov, Isaac, $d 1920-

740 01 Annotated Gilbert & Sullivan.

740 01 Asimov's annotated Gilbert and Sullivan.

Example 8

TITLE PAGE

A NEW BROOKLYN MUSEUM
The Master Plan Competition

Edited by
Joan Darragh

Foreword by
Robert T. Buck

Introduction by
Reyner Banham

The Brooklyn Museum
and
Rizzoli, New York

OTHER INFORMATION

The verso of the title page includes the following information:

Published for the exhibition
A NEW BROOKLYN MUSEUM: THE MASTER PLAN
 COMPETITION
March 11-July 4, 1988

Project Director: Joan Darragh

First published in the United States of America in 1988 by
Rizzoli International Publications

Copyright 1988 The Brooklyn Museum, New York

There are 214 pages with many illustrations; some are in color. The ISBN
is 0-8478-0863-7.

BOOKS WORKFORM

Leader   nam   a
Fixed Data 008
  Entrd: nnnnnn   Dat tp: Dates: Ctry: Illus:
  Int lvl: Repr: Cont: Govt pub: Conf pub: Festsch:
  Indx: M/E: Fict: Bio: Lang: Mod rec: Source:

020

041 _

1_ _ _

245 _ _

250

260 _

300

4_ _ _

5_

7_ _ _

7_ _ _

8_ _ _

Choice of entry: This work emanates from a corporate body, but the body cannot be the main entry because it does not fall into any of the categories under 21.1B2. So 21.7B1 applies, and entry is under title.

Darragh and the Museum are given added entries according to 21.30D1 and 21.30E1.

Description: The title and statement of responsibility are transcribed according to 2.1B1, 2.1E1, and 2.1F1. The publication information is transcribed according to 2.4B1, 1.4D5, and 2.4F1.

Physical description follows 2.5B2, 2.5C1, and 2.5D1. A note on the nature of the publication is given following 2.7B1.

The standard book number is included in the record following 2.8B1. However, it is included in field 020 as a string without spacing or punctuation, not in the way the rule directs.

Leader   nam   a
Fixed Data 008
  Entrd: nnnnnn Dat tp: s Dates: 1988,   Ctry: nyu Illus: a
  Int lvl: Repr: Cont: c Govt pub: Conf pub: 0 Festsch: 0
  Indx: 0 M/E: 0 Fict: 0 Bio: Lang: eng Mod rec: Source: d

020   0847808637

245 02 A New Brooklyn Museum : $b the master plan competition / $c edited by Joan Darragh ; foreword by Robert T. Buck ; introduction by Reyner Banham.

260 0 New York : $b Brooklyn Museum : $b Rizzoli, $c 1988.

300   214 p. : $b ill. ; $c 28 cm.

500   Catalog for an exhibition held Mar. 11-July 4, 1988.

700 10 Darragh, Joan.

710 20 Brooklyn Museum.

Example 9

TITLE PAGE

SANTA CRUZ COUNTY/CITY

LAW ENFORCEMENT

HELICOPTER PATROL PROGRAM

Prepared by

RESEARCH, PLANNING AND
DEVELOPMENT UNIT

ADMINISTRATION DIVISION
SANTA CRUZ POLICE DEPARTMENT

In Cooperation with the

Santa Cruz County Sheriff's Department
and Other Cities and Agencies in the County

April 1, 1973

OTHER INFORMATION

This is a typescript. There are 47 leaves, an appendix with leaves numbered A-1 to A-7, and the appendix is followed by two more leaves numbered 48 and 49 which are the bibliography. There are illustrations. The publication is 27.9 cm tall.

BOOKS WORKFORM

Leader   nam   a
Fixed Data 008
 Entrd: nnnnnn Dat tp: Dates: Ctry: Illus:
 Int lvl: Repr: Cont: Govt pub: Conf pub: Festsch:
 Indx: M/E: Fict: Bio: Lang: Mod rec: Source:

020

041 _

1__ __

245 __

250

260 _

300

4__ __

5__

7__ __

7__ __

8__ __

Choice of entry: This work is a work emanating from a corporate body and dealing with the operations of the body. Thus it meets the criteria in 21.1B2 for entry under the body. The Unit falls into Type 3 of the kinds of government agencies that are entered subordinately in 24.18A. The Police Department is included in the heading and the Administration Division is omitted from it according to 24.19A. The added entry for the Sheriff's Department is made according to 24.18A, Type 1. The elements of the heading for Santa Cruz and Santa Cruz County are made according to 23.2A1 and 23.4C2.

Department is abbreviated in the heading following LCRI for Appendix B.9.

Description: The title and statement of responsibility are transcribed according to 2.1B1 and 2.1F1. This work has the "look" of a published work though no explicit publisher's statement appears. The Unit which prepared it was assumed to have published it and the information was transcribed in brackets according to 2.4D1, 2.4E1, and 2.4F1.

There are two sequences of numbering, even though one is in the middle of the other. They are transcribed following 2.5B2. The rest of the physical description follows 2.5C1 and 2.5D1.

Leader   nam   a
Fixed Data 008
  Entrd: nnnnnn Dat tp: s Dates: 1973,   Ctry: cau Illus: a
  Int lvl: Repr: Cont: b Govt pub: 1 Conf pub: 0 Festsch: 0
  Indx: 0 M/E: 1 Fict: 0 Bio: Lang: eng Mod rec: Source: d

110 10 Santa Cruz (Calif.). $b Police Dept. $b Research, Planning and
Development Unit.

245 10 Santa Cruz County/City law enforcement helicopter patrol program / $c prepared
by Research, Planning and Development Unit, Administration Division, Santa Cruz Police
Department in cooperation with the Santa Cruz County Sheriff's Department and other
cities and agencies in the county.

260 0 [Santa Cruz : b The Unit, $c 1973]

300   49, 7 leaves : $b ill. ; $c 28 cm.

504   Includes bibliographical references (leaves 48-49)

710 10 Santa Cruz County (Calif.). $b Sheriff's Dept.

Example 10

ARTICLE TITLE CAPTION

THE WOMAN WARRIOR

ANN SIMONTON FIGHTS FOR FEMINIST ISSUES . . .

AND AGAINST THE SI SWIMSUIT ISSUE

by JILL LIEBER

OTHER INFORMATION

The caption above is at the beginning of an article in the February 1989 issue of *Sports Illustrated*. The number of the issue is v. 70, no. 6.

The article begins on page 132 and continues to page 134. There are pictures of Simonton as part of it. The magazine is 28 cm tall.

Simonton is a former model and founder of the Santa Cruz organization Media Watch.

Direct access to this article is desired for the public catalog.

BOOKS WORKFORM

Leader   naa   a
Fixed Data 008
  Entrd: nnnnnn Dat tp: Dates: Ctry: Illus:
  Int lvl: Repr: Cont: Govt pub: Conf pub: Festsch:
  Indx: M/E: Fict: Bio: Lang: Mod rec: Source:

041 _

1__ __ __
245 __ __

260 _
300
4__ __ __

5__
5__
7__ __ __

7__ __ __
773 _

Choice of entry: This is a work by a single personal author, and choice of entry is determined by 21.4A1. Form of heading is determined by 22.1, 22.4, 22.5A1.

Description: The title is transcribed according to 2.1B1; other title information, according to 2.1E1. The punctuation . . . is changed to — following 1.1B1. The statement of responsibility is transcribed according to 2.1F1.

Physical description is recorded following 2.5B6, 2.5C1, and 2.5D1.

Since there is no title page, source is title is recorded in a note following 2.7B3. A summary note was included to show the relationship to this geographic area, but that is optional. It is likely that some special relationship would exist before the analytic would be made.

Instead of a publication area, there is an "in-analytic" note constructed according to 13.5A. In a machine record, the note is tagged 773 and the subfield $7 precedes the other data.

Leader   naa   a
Fixed Data 008
  Entrd: nnnnnn Dat tp: s Dates: 1989   Ctry: xx Illus: c
  Int lvl: Repr: Cont: Govt pub: Conf pub: 0 Festsch: 0
  Indx: M/E: 1 Fict: 0 Bio: Lang: eng Mod rec: Source: d

100 10 Lieber, Jill.

245 14 The woman warrior : $b Ann Simonton fights for feminist issues-- and against the SI swimsuit issue / $c by Jill Lieber.

300   p. 132-134 : $b ports. ; $c 28 cm.

500   Caption title.

520 0 Ann Simonton, former model, and founder of the Santa Cruz (Calif.) organization Media Watch.

773 0 $7 nnas $t Sports illustrated. $g v. 70, no. 6 (February 1989).

ARCHIVAL AND MANUSCRIPTS CONTROL

Steven L. Hensen's *Archives, personal papers, and manuscripts : a cataloging manual for archival repositories, historical societies, and manuscript libraries (APPM)*, has come to be regarded as the standard for most archival bibliographic description. The second edition was published in 1989. The Library of Congress and the major utilities consider records prepared according to *APPM* to be fully compatible with *AACR2*.

Hensen's manual has been used to prepare the first three archival and manuscript records that follow. *AACR2R* has been used to prepare the fourth record. A library may choose to follow either standard. Machine coding conventions will vary in some fields, depending on which cataloging conventions are chosen.

Example 11

DESCRIPTION

The item is a carbon copy of a one-page typescript letter (8 1/2 x 11 in.) dated December 8, 1967. The letter is addressed as follows:

> President Lyndon B. Johnson
> The White House
> Washington, D.C.

The closing is as follows:

> Florence R. Wyckoff
> Mrs. Hubert Wyckoff
> Member,
> State Board of Public Health

Other documents in the collection indicate that the state is California. The carbon copy is unsigned.

Florence R. Wyckoff was active for more than 50 years in Santa Cruz County and at the state and national levels as an advocate for children and migrant families.

Wyckoff is writing to solicit Johnson's support for Senate bill (S-2388) and House bill (HR-12756) to extend the provisions of the Migrant Health Act scheduled to expire on June 30, 1968.

ARCHIVAL AND MANUSCRIPTS CONTROL WORKFORM

Leader   nbm   a
Fixed Data 008
  Entrd: nnnnnn Dat tp: Dates: ,   Ctry:
  Form of item: Lang: Mod rec: Source:

1__ _

245 _ _

260

300

5__

5__

5__

7__ _ _

Choice of entry: The choice of main entry for the letter written by Florence Wyckoff is made in accordance with *APPM* 2.1A5 (which is also in accord with *AACR2R* 21.1A2). The choice and form of the name are per *APPM* 3.2Ab, which says to choose the name by which the person is clearly most commonly known, and 3.5A. Florence Wyckoff does not always use "Mrs. Hubert Wyckoff" following her own name in her letters.

Description: The title is transcribed according to *APPM* 1.1B2, 1.1B4, 1.1B5, and 1.1E1. If *AACR2R* Chapter 4 were followed, the title would be recorded as follows: 245 00 [Letter] 1967 Dec. 8 [to] President Lyndon B. Johnson, Washington, D.C.

There is, of course, no place or publisher for this manuscript. The date area is not defined for archival materials (*APPM* 1.3).

The physical description follows *APPM* 1.5B1 and 1.5D2.

The "carbon copy" is not treated as the sort of "reproduction" dealt with in *APPM* 1.7B5. This carbon copy is presumably Wyckoff's own "original" copy of the letter sent to Johnson.

The 520 note is given in accord with *APPM* 1.7B2. The 545 note is required by *APPM* 1.7B1.

Leader   nbm   a
Fixed Data 008
  Entrd: nnnnnn   Dat tp: s   Dates: 1967,   Ctry: cau
  Form of item: Lang: eng   Mod rec: Source: d

100 1   Wyckoff, Florence R.

245 00   Letter : $b to President Lyndon B. Johnson, Washington, D.C., 1967 Dec. 8.

300   1 item (1 leaf) ; $c 28 cm.

500   Carbon copy (unsigned) of the original letter.

520   Wyckoff solicits Johnson's support for Senate bill (S-2388) and House bill
(HR-12756) to extend the provisions of the Migrant Health Act scheduled to expire on
June 30, 1968.

545   Florence R. Wyckoff was active for more than 50 years in Santa Cruz County and at
the state and national levels as an advocate for children and migrant families.

Example 12

DESCRIPTION

The item is known as the *San Simeon Guestbook*. It is an unpaged, one-volume, bound book, 38 cm. in height and 28 cm. in width. There is no printed information on the binding and there is no title page.

The book contains 11 pages of inscriptions by 11 guests of the Hearst family at Hearst Castle near San Simeon, California, written in 1931 and 1932, and a five-page holograph poem by William Randolph Hearst.

ARCHIVAL AND MANUSCRIPTS CONTROL WORKFORM

Leader   nbm   a
Fixed Data 008
  Entrd: nnnnnn Dat tp: Dates: ,   Ctry:
  Form of item: Lang: Mod rec: Source:

1__ _

245 _ _

260

300

5__

5__

5__

7__ _ _

Choice of entry: This *Guestbook* does not qualify for main entry under a personal author (i.e. Hearst) either under *APPM* or *AACR2R*. Entry is therefore under title (*APPM* 2.1C1). The author added entry for Hearst is provided because of the poem he wrote in the *Guestbook*. The form of the heading is per 3.2A and 3.5A.

Description: Since no title appears on the item, it is supplied, per *APPM* 1.1B2. The dates are recorded in the title area, per *APPM* 1.1B5. Similar examples would be the coverage dates of a diary or logbook. The physical description is given according to *APPM* 1.5B2 and 1.5D2. The 520 note is required by *APPM* 1.7B2.

Leader   nbm   a
Fixed Data 008
 Entrd: nnnnnn Dat tp: i Dates: 1931,1932 Ctry: cau
 Form of item: Lang: eng Mod rec: Source: d

245 00 San Simeon guestbook, $f 1931-1932.

300   1 v. (16 p.) ; $c 38 x 28 cm.

520   Inscriptions by eleven guests of the Hearst family at Hearst Castle near San Simeon, California, written in 1931 and 1932, and a five-page holograph poem by William Randolph Hearst.

700 10 Hearst, William Randolph, $d 1863-1951.

Example 13

DESCRIPTION

This collection consists of 37 boxes (40 linear ft.) of personal correspondence and papers of Clark Kerr as chancellor of the University of California, Berkeley, from 1952-1958 and President of the University of California from 1958-1967. The collection was given to the library by Clark Kerr as a gift in 1970. An unpublished finding aid to the collection is available in the Library.

ARCHIVAL AND MANUSCRIPTS CONTROL WORKFORM

Leader   nbc   a
Fixed Data 008
  Entrd: nnnnnn Dat tp: Dates: ,   Ctry:
  Form of item: Lang: Mod rec: Source:

1__ _

245 _ _

260

300

5__

5__

5__

7__ _ _

Choice of entry: This collection of personal correspondence and papers is entered under Kerr, according to *APPM* 2.1A1. This rule provides that the papers may be "by and/or to a given person."

Hensen's manual would provide for entry under Kerr, even if he were not the author of any of the papers in the collection. Hensen explains that "the responsibility for the intellectual content of . . . [archival materials] is directly related to archival principles of provenance rather than to the more deliberate creative relationship existing between books and their authors" (p. 39).

The form of the heading for Kerr is per 3.2A and 3.5A.

Description: The title is supplied by the cataloger, per *APPM* 1.1B2, 1.1B4, and the dates per 1.1B5. The statement of extent follows *APPM* 1.5B1. The 520 note is required by *APPM* 1.7B2. The information in the 541 field is recorded per *APPM* 1.7B10, which also states that local practices may preclude the expressing of such information in a publicly accessible catalog record. The 555 note regarding the finding aid is prescribed by *APPM* 1.7B13.

Leader   nbc   a
Fixed Data 008
  Entrd: nnnnnn Dat tp: i   Dates: 1958,1967 Ctry: cau
  Form of item: Lang: eng   Mod rec: Source: d

100 1 Kerr, Clark, $d 1911-

245 00 Papers, $f 1958-1967.

300   37 boxes (40 linear ft.)

520   Personal correspondence and papers of Clark Kerr as chancellor of the University of California, Berkeley, from 1952-1958 and President of the University of California from 1958-1967.

541   Clark Kerr $c gift $d 1970.

555   Unpublished finding aid available in the Library.

Example 14

TITLE PAGE

PRELIMINARY DRAFT

Streetpeople and Straightpeople in Santa Cruz, California
A Report of the Downtown Study

William H. Friedland, Ph.d.
Principal Investigator
Professor of Community Studies
and Sociology

Robert A. Marotto, Ph.d.
Research Director

April 1985

University of California, Santa Cruz
Division of Social Sciences

OTHER INFORMATION

This is a typescript. There are 69 leaves and then eleven appendices, each with its own foliation.

ARCHIVAL AND MANUSCRIPTS CONTROL WORKFORM

Leader   nbm   a
Fixed Data 008
 Entrd: nnnnnn Dat tp: Dates: ,   Ctry:
 Form of item: Lang: Mod rec: Source:

1__ _

245 _ _

260

300

5__

5__

5__

7__ _ _

It is necessary to decide whether material like this is published. The Division of Social Sciences is not the publisher. The report was prepared for the City of Santa Cruz and distributed in some way by it. Since the piece lacks indication that the work is published, it has been cataloged following the rules for manuscripts.

This work has been described according to *AACR2R* Chapter 4, rather than Hensen's manual (*APPM*).

Choice of entry: This is work of shared responsibility with principal responsibility indicated; so Friedland is the author. Choice of name and form of heading for both persons is determined by 22.1A, 22.4A, and 22.4B.

Description: Title proper, other title information, and statement of responsibility are transcribed according to 4.1B1, 4.1E1, and 4.1F1.

Preliminary draft constitutes an edition statement and is transcribed following 4.2B1. The abbreviation is done according to Appendix B.9.

The date of production is recorded following 4.4B1. Option applied and month added.

Since the book includes 12 separately paged sections, the physical description is done according to 2.5B9c, as instructed by 4.5B1.

If this work were described according to Hensen's manual, the statement of extent would be transcribed as *1 item* followed by the number of pages or leaves in parentheses (*APPM* 1.5B2).

```
Leader          nbm        a
Fixed Data 008
 Entrd: nnnnnn Dat tp: s  Dates: 1985,    Ctry: cau
 Form of item:      Lang: eng  Mod rec:    Source: d
```

100 1 Friedland, William H.

245 10 Streetpeople and straightpeople in Santa Cruz, California : $b a report
of the Downtown study / $c William H. Friedland, principal investigator ; Robert A.
Marotto, research director.

250   Prelim. draft.

260    $c 1985 Apr.

300   1 v. (various foliations) ; $c 28 cm.

700 10 Marotto, Robert A.

COMPUTER FILES

The chief source of information for computer files is the title screen or screens (9.0B1). *AACR2R* provides for the common problem of the cataloger not having access to equipment to read the file by permitting descriptive information to be taken from non-internal sources (label, accompanying material, non-integral container). The source of the title proper must *always* be given for computer files (9.7B3).

The cataloger has to exercise judgment regarding which is the predominant material when a computer file is issued with, for example, a book (1.10B). If the computer file is the primary item, then the book may be described as accompanying material (9.5E, 9.7B11).

Books or other printed materials that accompany computer files generally contain information regarding the system requirements of the file. This information is prescribed in 9.7B1 and is recorded in field 538.

There are a number of recently published manuals that are helpful to catalogers who must catalog computer files. Particularly noteworthy is Nancy B. Olson's *Cataloging Microcomputer Software*.

Example 15

TITLE SCREEN

> **The New Electronic Encyclopedia**
>
> **Grolier Electronic Publishing, Incorporated**
>
> **Danbury, Connecticut**
>
> **Copyright 1988**

OTHER INFORMATION

The encyclopedia text is carried on a compact disk, also known as a computer laser optical disk. This particular one is a "CD-ROM" (compact disk/read only memory). It is accompanied by one program disk (5 1/4 in. floppy) and a printed user's guide (35 pages, 27 cm.)

The user's guide states that the amount of memory required is 512K or greater; that the operating system required is DOS 3.0 or later; and that a compact disk player and a monitor are required. The guide also contains the statement: "All 21 volumes of the Academic American Encyclopedia on a single CD-ROM."

The following information is printed on the compact disk: The Electronic Encyclopedia for IBM PC and most compatibles.

COMPUTER FILES WORKFORM

Leader   nmm   a
Fixed Data 008
 Entrd: nnnnnn Dat tp: Dates: ,   Ctry: Frequn:
 Regulr: Type of File: Govt Pub:
 Lang: Mod rec: Source:

1__ _

245 _ _

260

300

538

5__

5__

5__

5__

7__ _ _

7__ _ _

7__ _ _

Choice of entry: There is no personal or corporate body responsibility stated in the item, so the main entry is the title (21.1C1). The added entry for Grolier is per 21.30E1, and the form of the heading is per 24.1A and 24.5C1. In accordance with 21.30G1, a title added entry (tagged 730) is made for the 21-volume related work. An added entry (tagged 740) is made for the variant title that appears on the disk label, in accordance with the last paragraph of 21.30J1.

Description: The cataloger judges that the compact disk is the predominant medium, so the other materials are treated as accompanying material. A compact disk on which computer files are recorded is cataloged according to Chapter 9. The chief source of information for computer files is the title screen(s). When the cataloger doesn't have access to equipment to read the file, the data is transcribed from the physical carrier (i.e., the disk) or its labels, or other external sources (9.0B1). For the present example, the cataloger is able to read the file from the title screen. The title proper is transcribed according to 9.1B1, and the general material designation follows it immediately, in accord with the LCRI for 9.1C.

The publication data follows 9.4C1, 9.4D1 (and 1.4D2), and 9.4F1. The physical description follows 9.5B1 and 9.5D1a. The accompanying material (program disk and user's guide) is described per 9.5E1.

The system requirements and disk characteristics information is transcribed in separate notes tagged 538 (9.7B1b and 9.7B10). The source of the title proper is given in a note (9.7B3). The variant title that appears on the CD ROM disk label is recorded in a note (9.7B4). The quoted information about the related work is also recorded in a note (9.7B7, and 1.7A3), which justifies the 740 title added entry described above.

Leader   nmm   a
Fixed Data 008
  Entrd: nnnnnn Dat tp: s Dates: 1988,   Ctry: ctu Frequn: n
  Regulr: Type of File: m Govt Pub:
  Lang: eng   Mod rec: Source: d

245 04 The New electronic encyclopedia $h [computer file]

260   Danbury, Conn. : $b Grolier Electronic Publishing, $c c1988.

300   1 computer laser optical disk ; $c 4 3/4 in. + $e 1 program disk ;
5 1/4 in. + 1 user's guide (35 p. ; 27 cm.)

538   System requirements: IBM PC and most compatibles; 512K memory or greater;
DOS 3.0 or later; CD ROM player; monitor.

538   Disk characteristics: CD-ROM.

500   Title from title screen.

500   Title on CD ROM disk: The electronic encyclopedia.

500   "All 21 volumes of the Academic American encyclopedia on a single
CD-ROM" -- User's guide.

710 20 Grolier Electronic Publishing.

730 01 Academic American encyclopedia.

740 01 Electronic encyclopedia.

Example 16

DESCRIPTION

The following items are issued in a case: four computer disks (floppy, 5 1/4 in.), and one workbook. The workbook has 170 pages, is illustrated and is 21 cm. in height. The cataloger does not have access to equipment to read the computer files.

The computer disk labels include the following information:

CBS SOFTWARE
For IBM PC and PCjr. 128K
c1984
Mastering the GRE No. 30310

WORKBOOK TITLE PAGE

Mastering the GRE

by Theodore Silver, J.D., M.D.

Programmed by Isaac Dimitrovsky

*"GRE" and "Graduate Record Examination" are registered trademarks of the College Entrance Examination Board. These materials have been prepared by CBS Software which bears sole responsibility for their contents.

CBS Software, A Unit of CBS Inc.,
Greenwich, Connecticut

OTHER INFORMATION

The cover of the workbook includes the following information: **For use with "Mastering the GRE" Computer Program.**

The verso of the workbook title page includes the following information:

c1984 by CBS Software
First printing September 1984
ISBN 0-03-830310-8

The following information is printed on the case: **You will need DOS 1.1, 2.0, or 2.1 to run the program. If you are using an IBM PCjr., use DOS 2.1 and a BASIC cartridge.**

COMPUTER FILES WORKFORM

Leader   nmm   a
Fixed Data 008
 Entrd: nnnnnn Dat tp: Dates: ,   Ctry: Frequn:
 Regulr: Type of File: Govt Pub:
 Lang: Mod rec: Source:

1__ _

245 _ _

260

300

538

5__

5__

5__

5__

7__ _ _

7__ _ _

7__ _ _

The cataloger judges that the computer disks are the dominant material and the workbook is accompanying material.

Choice of entry: This is a work of shared responsibility in which different persons have apparently prepared separate contributions, so 21.6b applies. Only two persons are named in the chief source of information. The cataloger judges that Silver is principally responsible because he is named first in larger typeface in the chief source of information (21.6B1). An added entry is made for the other contributor, per 21.6B1. The forms for the authors' names are per 22.1B and 22.5A1. The added entry for the corporate body is per 21.30E1, and the form is according to 24.1A and 24.4B1.

Description: The title is transcribed from the workbook (called the "documentation" in 9.0B1) because the most complete information appears there, and the cataloger doesn't have access to equipment to read the file. The general material designation is recorded after the title proper in accord with the LCRI for 9.1C. The statement of responsibility is per 9.1F1 and 1.1F7. The publication data is transcribed per 9.4C1, 9.4D1, and 9.4F1. The physical description for the computer files and workbook is per 9.5B1, 9.5D1a, 9.5D2, and 9.5E1.

The nature of the item and the system requirements for the file are recorded in the first two notes (9.7B1). This information may be taken from anywhere in the item. The source of the title is given per 9.7B3. The note regarding the number that appears on the disk labels is given per 9.8B2 and 9.7B19. The note describing the case is per 9.7B10.

Leader   nmm   a
Fixed Data 008
 Entrd: nnnnnn Dat tp: s Dates: 1984, Ctry: ctu Frequn: n
 Regulr: Type of File: u Govt Pub:
 Lang: eng Mod rec: Source: d

020 0038303108

100 10 Silver, Theodore.

245 10 Mastering the GRE $h [computer file] / $c by Theodore Silver ;
programmed by Isaac Dimitrosky.

260 Greenwich, Conn. : $b CBS Software, $c c1984.

300 4 computer disks ; $c 5 1/4 in. + $e 1 workbook (170 p. : ill. ; 21 cm.)

520 Designed to provide practice for the Graduate Record Examination.

538 System requirements: IBM PC with DOS 1.1, 2.0, or 2.1; IBM PCjr
with DOS 2.1 and BASIC cartridge; 128K; monitor.

500 Title from workbook.

500 On disk labels: no. 30310.

500 Issued in a case.

700 10 Dimitrovsky, Isaac.

710 20 CBS Software (Firm)

Example 17

DESCRIPTION

This group of materials consists of 11 computer disks (5 1/4'), a 57-page technical guide which is 30 cm. in height, a cable fitted with a 25 pin plug, and a 9/25 point plug adaptor. (A slip accompanying these materials lists each of the foregoing as components of the shipment.) The computer files were created as consultation software for a videodisc issued separately under the same title. The cataloger does not have equipment to mount and read the computer files.

The disk label includes the following information:

IMAGES DE LA REVOLUTION FRANCAISE

English version   Bibliotheque Nationale   Pergamon Press

OTHER INFORMATION

The title of the technical guide is: **Guide to the Installation and Use of "Revolution Software, 1989/1990".**

Page 5 of the technical guide contains the following:

"The software . . . is made up of a bibliographic database in either French or English and of a multi-function consultation program which is bilingual and can be set to different parameters. The software offers additional indexes over and above those contained in the printed catalogue published by the Bibliotheque Nationale. Besides multiple access for consultation (by the name of the collector, for example), the software offers an opportunity to cross criteria, to create picture selections, slide shows, personalised commentaries, etc."

The technical guide also contains the following information about what is needed to access the computer files:

"Equipment requirements are: an IBM PC, AT, PS or compatible with 640K RAM, a hard disk of at least 40 Mb, drive 1,2 Mb; monochrome or color video screen (MDA, Hercules, CGA, EGA or VGA); serial port to connect videodisc drive; parallel port to connect optional standard printer; Laservision videodisc drive to read the associated videodisc."

COMPUTER FILES WORKFORM

Leader   nmm   a
Fixed Data 008
  Entrd: nnnnnn   Dat tp: Dates: ,   Ctry: Frequn:
  Regulr: Type of File: Govt Pub:
  Lang: Mod rec: Source:

1__ _

245 _ _

260

300

538

5__

5__

5__

5__

7__ _ _

7__ _ _

7__ _ _

The cataloger judges that the computer files are the predominant component. The other materials are described as accompanying material.

Choice of entry: This work is entered under its title, in accordance with 21.1C1c. The added entry for the Bibliotheque Nationale is made per 21.30E; its form is per 24.1A and 24.4C2.

Description: Since the cataloger doesn't have the equipment to read the file, the chief source of information will be the disk label, in accord with 9.0B1. The title is transcribed per 9.1B1, and a note on the source of the title is transcribed per 9.7B3. The general material designation is added after the title proper in accord with the LCRI for 9.1C. The edition statement is per 9.2B. Publication data is recorded per 1.4C6, 1.4D5, and 1.4F7. The physical description is per 9.5B1, 9.5D1, and 9.5E1. The notes are prescribed by 9.7B1a and b, 9.7B3, and 9.7B4.

Leader   nmm   a
Fixed Data 008
  Entrd: nnnnnn Dat tp: s Dates: 1990,   Ctry: fr   Frequn: n
  Regulr: Type of File: m Govt Pub:
  Lang: eng   Mod rec: Source: d

245 0 0 Images de la Revolution francaise $h [computer file]

250   English version.

260   [Paris?] : $b Bibliotheque nationale ; $a [s.l.] : $b Pergamon Press, $c [1990?]

300   11 computer disks ; $c 5 1/4 in. + $e 1 technical guide (57 p. ; 30 cm.) + 1 cable fitted with 25 pin plug + 1 9/25 point plug adaptor.

520   Consultation software for the videodisc of the same title.

500   "The software ... is made up of a bibliographic database in either French or English and of a multi-function consultation program which is bilingual and can be set to different parameters. The software offers additional indexes over and above those contained in the printed catalogue published by the Bibliotheque Nationale. Besides multiple access for consultation (by the name of the collector, for example), the software offers an opportunity to cross criteria, to create picture selections, slide shows, personalised commentaries, etc." -- Technical guide, p. 5.

538   System requirements: IBM PC, AT, PS or compatible; 640K RAM; hard disk of at least 40 Mb; drive 1,2 Mb; monochrome or color video screen (MDA, Hercules, CGA, EGA or VGA) ; serial port to connect videodisc drive; parallel port to connect optional standard printer; Laservision videodisc drive to read the associated videodisc.

500   Title from disk label.

500   Accompanying technical guide has title: Technical guide to the installation and use of "Revolution software, 1989/1990."

710 20 Bibliotheque nationale (France)

740 01 Technical guide to the installation and use of "Revolution software, 1989/1990."

740 01 Images of the French Revolution.

MAPS

Cartographic materials of all sorts are covered in *AACR2R* Chapter 4. The nonspecialist cataloger who must catalog such materials will discover two problem areas. The first has to do with choice of main entry. The second involves the elements of the mathematical area of description (e.g., *scale, projection, coordinates*, etc.).

Margaret F. Maxwell's *Handbook for AACR2, 1988 Revision* provides an informative introduction to the controversies in map cataloging. The problem of the authorship principle in relation to cartographic materials seems not to have been solved to the satisfaction of map librarians. Who is responsible for the intellectual content of the map? The cartographer? The surveyor? The publisher? The government agency issuing the map? *AACR2R* leaves it to the cataloger to determine whether a person named on the map qualifies as personal author under 21.1A1. Rule 21.1B2f does make special provision for corporate body main entry for cartographic materials. It is restricted, however, to bodies that are responsible for more than simply the publication or distribution of the materials. Many cartographic materials will be entered under title (21.1C1).

For the problem of technical knowledge needed to complete the mathematical area (3.3), Maxwell recommends *Cartographic Materials: A Manual of Interpretation for AACR2*, which helps illuminate some of those mysteries. This manual is also very helpful in determining both the chief source of information and the main entry for an item.

In USMARC, the Geographic Classification Code field (052) is mandatory for the maps format. Data are entered in a combination of numeric and alphanumeric codes that represent geographic area and subarea. These codes are based on authoritative agency lists. The geographic area code is derived from the *Library of Congress—Class G* and expanded Cutter number lists for place names. In most implementations, the code is assigned when a subject heading for the work contains a geographic term. The third map exercise in this workbook contains a code derived from the title information alone.

Example 18

TITLE PAGE

CALIFORNIA WIND ATLAS

Prepared for the California Energy Commission

by the

California Department of Water Resources

Scale 1:600,000

Sacramento, California

California Energy Commission

1985

OTHER INFORMATION

The cover title is California Energy Commission Wind Atlas.

This atlas contains vi, 210 pages; some of the maps are colored, and the size is 28 cm. In a pocket there are 4 folded map plates with the titles: Wind measurement sites, Mean annual wind speed in California (North), Mean annual wind speed in California (South), and Electric transmission system.

MAPS WORKFORM

Leader
Fixed Data 008   nem   a
 Entrd: nnnnnn Dat tp: Dates: ,   Ctry: Relief:
 Project: Prime merid: MatType: Govt Pub:
 Indx: Form: Lang: Mod rec   Source:

034 _

1__ _

245 _ _

255

260 _

300

5__

5__

7__ _ _

7__ _ _

Choice of entry: The corporate body which prepared the atlas is the main entry, in accordance with 21.1B2f. The form of the main entry heading is per 24.18A (Type 1). An added entry for the Commission is prescribed in 21.30E1, and its form is established per 24.17A. The added entry for the cover title is prescribed in 21.30J1.

Description: The cataloger uses Chapter 3, Cartographic Materials, to describe an atlas of maps. The sources of information for a printed atlas, however, are the same as those for a book (2.0B). Both Chapter 2 and 3 must therefore be consulted to describe this item.

The title and statement of responsibility are transcribed per 2.1B1 and 2.1F1. The stated scale is transcribed following 3.3B1. The publication data is given per 3.4C1, 3.4D1, and 3.4F. The publisher is recorded in a shortened form, following 1.4D4. The physical description is given according to 3.5B3, 3.5C3, and 3.5D2. The note for the cover title is prescribed in 3.7B4. The maps in a pocket are described per 3.7B11.

Unlike other cartographic materials, an atlas is entered in the Books format in some implementations of USMARC (e.g. OCLC/MARC).

Leader
Fixed Data 008   nem   a
  Entrd: nnnnnn Dat tp: s Dates: 1985,   Ctry: cau Relief:
  Project: Prime merid: MatType: a   Govt Pub: s
  Indx: Form: Lang: eng Mod rec   Source: d

034 1 $b 6000000

110 10 California. $b Dept. of Water Resources.

245 10 California wind atlas / $c prepared for the California Energy Commission by the California Department of Water Resources.

255   Scale 1:600,000

260 0   Sacramento, CA : $b The Commission, $c 1985.

300   1 atlas (vi, 210 p.) $b ill., maps (some col.) ; $c 28 cm.

500   Cover title: California Energy Commission wind atlas.

500   Four folded map plates in pocket: Wind measure sites, Mean annual wind speed in California (North), Mean annual wind speed in California (South), Electric transmission system.

710 20 California Energy Commission.

740 01 California Energy Commission wind atlas.

Example 19

MAP PANEL

Rand McNally Map of California

Scale 1:1,298,880

Rand McNally & Co., Chicago

Copyright 1980

OTHER INFORMATION

The data above appears in a panel on the map. The title within the map margin is: California.

On the verso of the face of the map are other maps for: Sacramento, San Diego & vicinity, Metropolitan San Francisco, Metropolitan Los Angeles.

The maps are in color, and their collective size is 83 x 55 cm. The sheet on which they are printed measures 46 x 87 cm., folded to 23 x 11 cm.

Also printed on the verso are: Indexes, a descriptive index to points of interest, recreation facility index, distance list, colored illustrations, and an "Expense record."

MAPS WORKFORM

Leader
Fixed Data 008   nem   a
 Entrd: nnnnnn Dat tp: Dates: ,   Ctry: Relief:
 Project: Prime merid: MatType: Govt Pub:
 Indx: Form: Lang: Mod rec   Source:

034 _

1 __ _

245 _ _

255

260 _

300

5 __

5 __

7 __ _ _

7 __ _ _

Choice of entry: The main entry is under the map company that produced the map, per 21.1B2f. The form of that entry varies from the form that is printed in the panel. The established form is from the LC Names Authority File and is the one by which the company is commonly identified (24.1A). The title added entries are given per 21.30J.

Description: Presentation of bibliographical data on maps is not as standardized as it is on published books. The chief source for a cartographic item is the item itself or, failing that, its container (3.0B2). According to 3.1B3, if the item bears more than one title and the sequence or layout of the titles is insufficient to enable the choice to be made, the most comprehensive title is to be transcribed as the title proper. The panel title is the most comprehensive for this map. Rule 3.7B3 says to make a note on the source of title, and 3.7B4 says to make a note on other titles borne by the item.

The stated map scale is recorded per 3.3B1. Publication data is given per rule 3.4. The physical description follows 3.5B1, 3.5C3, and 3.5D1.

The note regarding the "relief" feature is recorded per 3.7B1. (*Spot heights* are defined in the manual cited at the beginning of the Maps section in this workbook.)

The notes describing the verso of the map are prescribed by 3.7B18.

Leader
Fixed Data 008   nem   a
  Entrd: nnnnnn Dat tp: s Dates: 1980,   Ctry: ilu Relief: g
  Project: Prime merid: MatType: a   Govt Pub:
  Indx: 1   Form: Lang: eng Mod rec   Source: d

034 1 $b 1298880

110 2 Rand McNally and Company.

245 10 Rand McNally map of California.

255   Scale 1:1,298,880.

260 0 Chicago : $b Rand McNally & Co., $c c1980.

300   1 map : $b col. ; $c 83 x 55 cm., on sheet 46 x 87 cm., folded to 23 x 11 cm.

500   Panel title.

500   Title within margin: California.

500   Relief shown by spot heights.

500   Indexes, descriptive index to points of interest, recreation facility index, distance list, col. ill., and "Expense record" on verso.

500   On verso: Sacramento -- San Diego & vicinity -- Metropolitan San Francisco -- Metropolitan Los Angeles.

740 01 Map of California.

740 01 California.

GEOLOGIC MAP OF THE SAN ANDREAS FAULT IN THE PARKFIELD 7.5-MINUTE QUADRANGLE, MONTEREY AND FRESNO COUNTIES, CALIFORNIA

By John D. Sims

1990

Example 20

MAP TITLE

Printed at the top of the sheet:

DEPARTMENT OF THE INTERIOR   MISCELLANEOUS FIELD STUDIES

U.S. GEOLOGICAL SURVEY   MAP MF-2115

DESCRIPTION

Printed at the bottom of the map portion is: **Transverse Mercator Projection . . . Scale 1:24000 . . . Geology mapped in 1983-86.** Relevant coordinates printed on the map corners are: **W 120 30 00, W 120 22 30, N 36 00 00, N 35 52 30.** In the lower righthand corner of the sheet is printed: **Interior--Geological Survey, Reston, VA--1990. For sale by U.S. Geological Survey, Map Distribution, Box 25286, Federal Center, Denver, CO 89225.** The map is printed in black and white; the relief is shown on the map by means of contours and spot heights.

The title data above appears along the bottom of a sheet 106 x 112 cm., printed on one side, and folded in an envelope 30 x 24 cm. On the printed side of the sheet is a map that measures 58 x 47 cm., some text, a bibliography, a table, an index, location maps, and 3 cross sections.

MAPS WORKFORM

Leader   nem   a
Fixed Data 008
 Entrd: nnnnnn Dat tp: Dates: ,   Ctry: Relief:
 Project: Prime merid: MatType: Govt Pub:
 Indx: Form: Lang: Mod rec   Source:

034 _

1__ _

245 _ _

255

260 _

300

5__

5__

7__ _ _

7__ _ _

Choice of entry: The corporate body which prepared the map is chosen as the main entry, in accordance with 21.1B2f and the LCRI for that rule. The U.S. Geological Survey, the body from which this map emanates, is judged to be chiefly responsible for the intellectual content, even though an individual (the cartographer? or the author of the text printed on the sheet?) is prominently named. See also the LCRI for 21.1B2 for a discussion of determining whether the main entry heading should be under a corporate body or a personal author when both are named.

The form of the main entry heading is per 24.17, which refers the cataloger to 24.1 since the corporate body does not fall under the types listed in 24.18. The qualifier is added to the heading in accordance with 24.4C2. (While the form of the name presented on this map is "U.S. Geological Survey," the cataloger will discover that the LC Authority File treats that form as a variant form from which a cross reference is made to "Geological Survey (U.S.)," the authoritative form.) An added entry for the personal author is made in accordance with 21.30B1; the form of this heading is per 22.1A and B. The added entry for a variant form of the title is justified by 21.30J (last paragraph). This entry is helpful in online catalogs with derived search keys (such as the OCLC database), where there may be many entries that begin "Geologic map of the . . ."

Description: Only one title is presented on the map sheet, and it is transcribed per 3.1B1. The statement of responsibility is recorded per 3.1F1. The name of the governmental mapping agency is also recorded here since it is known that the agency has contributed to the intellectual content of the map. The scale and related information is recorded per 3.3B1, 3.3C1. The LCRI for 3.3D says that LC applies the option, so the coordinates are transcribed per 3.3.D1. Publication data is transcribed per 3.4C1, 3.4D1, and 3.4F1. The physical description follows 3.5B1, 3.5D1, and the LCRI for 3.5D5. The series is recorded per 3.6B1. The notes are prescribed by 3.7B1 and 3.7B18.

Leader   nem   a
Fixed Data 008
  Entrd: nnnnnn Dat tp: s Dates: 1990,   Ctry: vau Relief: ag
  Project: bh Prime merid: MatType: a   Govt Pub: f
  Indx: 1   Form: Lang: eng Mod rec   Source: d

007   aj aanzn

034 1   a $b 24000 $d W1203000 $e W1202230 $f N0360000 $g N0355230

110 20 Geological Survey (U.S.)

245 10 Geologic map of the San Andreas Fault in the Parkfield 7.5-minute quadrangle, Monterey and Fresno counties, California / $c by John Sims ; Department of the Interior, U.S. Geological Survey.

255   Scale: 1:24,000 ; $b universal transverse Mercator proj. $c
(W 120 30 00 --W 120 22 30 /N 36 00 00 --N 35 52 30)

260 0   Reston, VA : $b The Survey ; $a Denver, CO : $b For sale by Map Distribution, $c 1990.

300   1 map ; $c 58 x 47 cm., on sheet 106 x 112 cm., folded in envelope 30 x 24 cm.

440 0 Miscellaneous field studies ; $v map MF-2115

500   Relief shown by contours and spot heights.

500   "Geology mapped in 1983-86."

500   Includes text, bibliography, table, index and location maps, and 3 cross sections.

700 10 Sims, John D.

740 01 San Andreas Fault in the Parkfield 7.5-minute quadrangle, Monterey and Fresno counties, California, geologic map of.

MUSIC & SOUND RECORDINGS

The special rules for the description of music are in Chapter 5; those for sound recordings are in Chapter 6. The special rules that apply for entry of musical works are 21.18 to 21.22. Those for sound recordings are 21.23 to 21.24. The rules for formulating uniform titles for musical works are 25.25 to 25.35. The rules for sound recording cover spoken work recordings as well as musical ones.

Example 21

COMPACT DISC LABEL

EMI

RAVEL

a)BOLERO
b)DAPHNIS ET CHLOE--Suite No. 2
c)PAVANE POUR UNE INFANTE DEFUNTE

STEREO
CDC
7471662
p1980

LONDON SYMPHONY ORCHESTRA
conducted by ANDRE PREVIN

OTHER INFORMATION

The disc is 4 3/4 in. in diameter. A booklet that is 10 pages long and 12 cm high is included. The notes in the booklet give historical information on the three works in English, German and French. The last page of the booklet includes the information that EMI made the original recording in 1980, but it was remastered digitally in 1984. The notes also give the location of EMI Records Ltd. as Hayes Middlesex England. It also includes the times of each of the works: 17'13', 17'09', and 6'40', respectively.

SOUND RECORDING WORKFORM

Leader   njm   a
Fixed Data 008
  Entrd: nnnnnn Dat tp: Dates: Ctry: Comp:
  Format: Audience: Form of item: Accomp mat:
  LitText: M/E: Lang: Mod rec: Source:

007

020

028 _ _

047

041 _

1_ _ _ _

245 _ _ _

260 _

300

4_ _ _ _

5_ _

5_ _

7_ _ _ _

7_ _ _ _

8_ _ _ _

Choice of entry: The choice of main entry is determined by 21.23B1, also calls for added entries for the principal performers. Choice of name for both Ravel and Previn is determined by 22.1A; form of heading, by 22.4A, 22.5A1, and 22.17A (option). The choice and form of the entry for the orchestra is determined by 24.1A. The codes used in $4 of the performer added entries are found in the publication *USMARC Code List for Relators, Sources, Description Conventions*.

The LCRI for 25.34B-C instructs the cataloger to make a collective uniform title for a recording containing three to five works by the same composer and then to make analytical added entries for each work. The collective uniform title is made following 25.34C1 and 25.34C3. The uniform title for the first work is constructed according to 25.27A1, 25.29A, 25.30A1, 25.30B1, 25.30B6. While a bolero is a type of composition, the singular is used because Ravel wrote only one work of the type. The uniform title for the second work is constructed according to 25.32A1 and 25.27A1. Suites are not strictly parts of works, but the rules for parts are used to make the uniform title. The examples following 25.32A1 do not exactly cover this case since both the name and number of the part are required for accurate identification. Also, there is no provision here to use the plural for titles that consist only of a form of composition. The uniform title for the third work is according to 25.27A1 and, since the work was composed originally for piano, 25.35C1. The LCRI for 21.30M1 calls for the inclusion of the date of publication in an analytical entry.

Description: Since the disc lacks a collective title, the titles of the individual works are transcribed following 6.1G2. The general material designation is given following 6.1C. It follows the last title as in the examples folowing 1.1G3 and 6.1G2. The statement of responsibility is transcribed following 6.1F1.

The publication information is transcribed according to 6.4C1, 6.4D1, and 6.4F1. 6.0B2 provides that among the prescribed sources for this information is the accompanying textual material; so information found there is not bracketed.

Physical description follows 6.5B1, 6.5B2, 6.5C2, 6.5C7, and 6.5D2. The LCRI for 6.5B2 says that, if the total playing time is not given but the durations of its parts are, the cataloger may add the stated durations together and round off to the next minute. Rather than describing the program notes as accompanying material as is possible following 6.5E1, the LCRI for 1.5E1 has been applied and they are described in a note, since they are of little bibliographic importance.

Leader   njm   a
Fixed Data 008
 Entrd: nnnnnn Dat tp: p Dates: 1984,1980 Ctry: enk Comp: mu
 Format: n Audience: Form of item: Accomp mat: i
 LitText: n M/E: 1 Lang: N/A Mod rec: Source: d

007 sd fzngnn e

028 02 CDC 7471622 $b EMI

041 0 $g engfreger

047 df $a su $a pv

048 oa

100 10 Ravel, Maurice, $d 1875-1937.

240 10 Orchestra music. $k Selections

245 00 Bolero ; Daphis et Chloe : suite no. 2 ; Pavane pour une infante defunte $h [sound recording] / $c Ravel.

260 0 Hayes, Middlesex, England : $b EMI, $c 1984.

300 1 sound disc (42 min.) : $b digital, stereo. ; 4 3/4 in.

511 0 London Symphony Orchestra, Andre Previn, conductor.

500 The 3rd work originally for piano.

500 Program notes in English, French and German (10 p.) inserted in container.

500 Durations: 17:13, 17:09, 6:40.

700 12 Ravel, Maurice, $d 1875-1937. $t Bolero. $f 1984.

700 12 Ravel, Maurice, $d 1875-1937. $t Daphnis et Chloe. $p Suite, $n no. 2. $f 1984.

700 12 Ravel, Maurice, $d 1875-1937. $t Pavane pour une infante defunte; $o arr. $f 1984.

700 10 Previn, Andre, $d 1929- $4 cnd

710 20 London Symphony Orchestra. $4 prf

Notes are given following 6.7B1, 6.7B6, 6.7B7, 6.7B10, and 6.7B11. Rather than giving the publisher's number in a note following 6.7B19, the information in included in field 028, which can be used to generate a note.

Example 22

COMPACT DISC LABEL

PROKOVIEV

1) Peter & the Wolf [27:22]
Andre Previn, Narrator

TELARC
DIGITAL

CD-80126
compact disc
digital audio
c1986 TELARC

Andre Previn

Royal Philharmonic Orchestra

BRITTEN

2) Young Person's Guide to the Orchestra [17:08]
3) Gloriana: Courtly Dances [10:18]

OTHER INFORMATION

The disc is 4 3/4 in. in diameter. It is accompanied by program notes that give historical information on the works and the text of Peter & the Wolf in English. The notes have 11 numbered pages and are 12 cm. tall. The notes have the information that the recording is in stereo and that it was made in Watford Town Hall, London, on November 20 & 21, 1985. They give the address of TELARC as Cleveland, Ohio.

SOUND RECORDING WORKFORM

Leader   njm   a
Fixed Data 008
  Entrd: nnnnnn Dat tp: Dates: Ctry: Comp:
  Format: Audience: Form of item: Accomp mat:
  LitText: M/E: Lang: Mod rec: Source:

007

020

028 _ _

047

041 _

1__ _ _

245 _ _

260 _

300

4__ _ _

5__

5__

7__ _ _

7__ _ _

8__ _ _

Choice of entry: The choice of main entry is determined by 21.23D1b, which says the entry should be the heading appropriate to the first work. Since the first work is a composition with words, 21.19A1 applies and calls for entry under the heading for the composer. Choice of name for Prokofiev is determined by 22.1A and 22.3C2. The LCRI for 22.3C2 says to apply the alternative rule and choose the form that has become well established in English language reference sources. Form of entry is determined by 22.4A, 22.5A1, and 22.17A (option). 21.23D1b also calls for added entries for the other works and for the principal performers. Choice of name for Britten and Previn is determined by 22.1A; form of heading, by 22.4A, 22.5A1, and 22.17A (option). The choice and form of the entry for the orchestra is determined by 24.1A. The relator codes used in $4 of the performer added entries are found in *USMARC Code List for Relators, Sources, Description Conventions*.

The uniform title for the first work is constructed according to 25.27A1 and 25.35F1. The uniform title for the second work follows 25.27A1 and for the third, 25.32.A1 and 25.27A1. The authoritative form of title is *Choral dances* rather than *Courtly dances*. Dates are added to these analytical entries following the LCRI for 21.30M1.

Description: Lacking a collective title, the titles of the individual works are transcribed following 6.1G2. The title of the Courtly Dances is transcribed following 1.1B9. The general material designation is given following 6.1C. It follows the last statement of responsibility as in the examples following 1.1G3 and 6.1G2. The statements of responsibility are transcribed following 6.1F1.

The publication information is transcribed according to 6.4C1, 6.4D1, and 6.4F1. 6.0B2 provides that among the prescribed sources for this information is the accompanying textual material; so information found there is not bracketed.

Physical description follows 6.5B1, 6.5B2, 6.5C2, 6.5C7, and 6.5D2. The LCRI for 6.5B2 says that, if the total playing time is not given but the durations of its parts are, the cataloger may add the stated durations together and round off to the next minute. Rather than describing the program notes as accompanying material as is possible following 6.5E1, the LCRI for 1.5E1 has been applied and they are described in a note, since they are of little bibliographic importance.

Notes are given following 6.7B6, 6.7B7, and 6.7B11. Rather than giving the publisher's number in a note following 6.7B19, it is included in field 028, which can be used to generate a note.

Leader   njm   a
Fixed Data 008
  Entrd: nnnnnn Dat tp: p Dates: 1986,1985 Ctry: ohu Comp: mu
  Format: n Audience: Form of item: Accomp mat: di
  LitText: n M/E: 1 Lang: eng Mod rec: Source: d

007   sd fzngnn e

028 02 CD-80126 $b Telarc

041 1 $d eng $h rus $e eng $g eng

047   vr $a zz

048   oa $b vn

100 10 Prokofiev, Sergey, $d 1891-1953.

240 10 Petia i volk. $l English

245 10 Peter & the wolf / $c Prokoviev. Young person's guide to the orchestra ;
Gloriana. $p Courtly dances / Britten $h [sound recording]

260 0   Cleveland, Ohio : $b Telarc, $c 1986, p1985.

300   1 sound disc (55 min.) : $b digital, stereo. ; $c 4 3/4 in.

511 0   Royal Philharmonic Orchestra, Andre Previn, conductor and narrator.

500   Program notes and English text of the 1st work (11 p.) inserted in container.

518   Recorded in Watford Town Hall, London, on Nov. 20 & 21, 1985.

700 12 Britten, Benjamin, $d 1913-1976. $t Young person's guide to the orchestra. $f 1986.

700 12 Britten, Benjamin, $d 1913-1976. $t Gloriana. $p Choral dances. $f 1986.

700 10 Previn, Andre, $d 1929- $4 cnd

710 20 Royal Philharmonic Orchestra. $4 prf

Example 23

COMPACT DISC LABEL

Alasdair Fraser
and Paul Machlis

Sona Gaia
ND-62755

THE ROAD NORTH

1 **Laughing Wolf/Mountain Madness** 3:10
   (Machlis) (Fraser)

2 **Traditional Gaelic Melody** 3:13 (Trad.)

3 **Tommy's Tarbukas** 2:29 (Fraser)

4 **Bennachie Sunrise/Willie's Trip to Toronto** 6:02
   (Machlis) (Holland)

5 **Slow Train** 5:13 (Machlis)

6 **Invercassley Falls/Trip to Ballyshannon** 4:05
   (Machlis) (Fraser)

7 **Calliope House/The Cowboy Jig** 3:49
   (Richardson) (Trad.)

8 **Bovaglie's Plaid** 3:48 (J.S. Skinner)

9 **The Banks of Spey/Brenda Stubbert's Reel** 3:50
   (Marshall) (Holland)

10 **The Road North** 4:12 (Fraser)

p 1989 Sona Gaia Productions, Inc.
P.O. Box 2740, Ukiah, CA USA
Distributed by MCA Distributing Corp. 70 Universal City Plaza
Universal City, CA USA

OTHER INFORMATION

A leaflet in the container includes the following information:
   Alasdair Fraser: Fiddle, viola
   Paul Machlis: Grand piano, synthesizer (both Yamaha)
   Michael O'Domhnaill: Guitar
   Tommy Hayer: Bodhran, tarbukas, bendir, friction drum
   Glen Moore: String bass

Recorded November 1987 and January 1988 at
Nightnoise Studios, Portland, OR

SOUND RECORDING WORKFORM

Leader   njm   a
Fixed Data 008
  Entrd: nnnnnn   Dat tp: Dates: Ctry: Comp:
  Format: Audience: Form of item: Accomp mat:
  LitText: M/E: Lang: Mod rec: Source:

007

020

028 _ _

047

041 _

1_ _ _

245 _ _

260 _

300

4_ _ _

5_

5_

7_ _ _

7_ _ _

8_ _ _

Choice of entry: This is a collection of works by different persons and there are two principal performers. Following 21.23C1, Fraser is the main entry and there is an added entry for Machlis. The form of heading for both names is determined by 22.1A, 22.4A, 22.5A.

Description: The title is transcribed according to 6.1B1. The *GMD sound recording* is added following 6.1C1 as Library of Congress does. Since Fraser's and Machlis's contribution goes beyond performance, their names are transcribed in the statement of responsibility following 6.1F1.

The publisher is transcribed according to 6.4C1, 6.4D1, 6.4E1, and 6.4F1.

The performers are listed according to 6.7B6; the history of the recording, according to 6.7B7. Since the date of recording and the date of publication differ, the date type in the 008 is *p* and the earliest date of recording is given as the second date. Contents, including statement of responsibility and duration, are recording following 6.7B18. The publisher's number is given in the 028 rather than the note called for in 6.7B19.

Leader   njm   a
Fixed Data 008
  Entrd: nnnnnn Dat tp: p Dates: 1989,1987 Ctry: cau Comp: mu
  Format: n Audience: Form of item: Accomp mat:
  LitText: n M/E: 1 Lang: eng Mod rec: Source: d

007   sd fzngnn   e

028 02 ND-62755 $b Sona Gaia

047   fm $a pp

100 10 Fraser, Alasdair.

245 14 The road north $h [sound recording] / $c Alasdair Fraser and Paul Machlis.

260 0   Ukiah, CA : $b Sona Gaia ; $a Universal City, CA : $b Distributed by MCA Distributing Corp, $c c1989.

300   1 sound disc (41 min.) : $b digital, stereo. ; $c 4 1/2 in.

511 0   Fraser, fiddle, viola ; Machlis, piano, synthesizer ; with supporting instrumentalists.

518   Recorded Nov. 1987 and Jan. 1988 at Nightnoise Studios, Portland, OR.

505 0   Laughing wolf/Mountain madness / Machlis, Fraser (3:10) -- Traditional Gaelic melody (3:13) -- Tommy's tarbukas / Fraser (2:29) -- Bennachie sunrise/Willie's trip to Toronto / Machlis, Holland (6:02) -- Slow train / Machlis (5:31) -- Invercassley Falls/Trip to Ballyshannon / Machlis, Fraser (4:05) -- Calliope House/The cowboy jig / Richardson, trad. (3:49) -- Bovaglie's plaid / J.K. Skinner (3:48) -- The banks of Spey/Brenda Stubbert's reel / Marshall, Holland (3:50) -- The road north / Fraser (4:12)

700 10 Machlis, Paul.

Example 24

SOUND RECORDING LABEL

"801 LIVE"

LAGRIMA (Manzanera) TNK (TOMORROW NEVER KNOWS)
(Lennon/McCartney) EAST OF ASTEROID (Manzanera,
MacCormick) RONGWRONG (Hayward) SOMBRE REPTILES
(Eno)

Produced by 801 for E.G. Records Ltd.,
Engineered by Rhett Davies

STEREO
28 151 XOT

28 151-A
STEMRA
Made in Holland

PHIL MANZANERA/ENO/BILL MacCORMICK/
FRANCIS MONKMAN/LLOYD WATSON/
SIMON PHILLIPS

P 1976 Island Records Ltd.

ARIOLA-EURODISC-BENELUX B.V. HAARLEM

Side 2 label is identical to Side 1 except for the contents, which follow:

BABY'S ON FIRE (Eno) DIAMOND HEAD (Manzanera)
MISS SHAPIRO (Manzanera, Eno) YOU REALLY GOT ME
(Davies) THIRD UNCLE (Eno)

OTHER INFORMATION

The container lists the following information:

PERSONNEL
Phil Manzanera - Guitar
Eno - Vocals/Synthesizer/Guitar/Tapes
Bill MacCormick - Bass/Vocals
Francis Monkman - Fender Rhodes/Clavinet
Simon Phillips - Drums/Rhythm Box
Lloyd Watson - Slide Guitar/Vocals

Recorded in the Queen Elizabeth hall
Live on the Island Mobile, September 3rd, 1976
Mixed at Basing Street Studios

All arrangements by 801
Produced by 801 for E.G. Records Ltd.

SOUND RECORDING WORKFORM

Leader   njm   a
Fixed Data 008
 Entrd: nnnnnn Dat tp: Dates: Ctry: Comp:
 Format: Audience: Form of item: Accomp mat:
 LitText: M/E: Lang: Mod rec: Source:

007

020

028 _ _

047

041 _

1__ _ _

245 _ _

260 _

300

4__ _ _

5__

5__

7__ _ _

7__ _ _

8__ _ _

Choice of entry: *801* is a musical group. The songs on this album were written by various members of the group and then performed by it. Thus, this disc meets the requirements in 21.1B2e for entry under the group as a corporate body. The form of entry is determined by 24.1A and 24.4B1 which calls for an addition to a corporate name that does not convey the idea of a corporate body.

Description: The title is transcribed according to 6.1B1 and the GMD added according to 6.1C1. The names of the members of the group are *not* given in the statement of responsibility following 6.1F2. It is not necessary to give this information in a note.

The publication information is transcribed following 1.4C6, 6.4D1, 6.4F1. Haarlem applies to Ariola-Eurodisc but cannot be taken for the place where Island Records is located. An alternative to *[S.l.]* would be *[Holland?]*. Physical description follows 6.5B1, 6.5C2-3, 6.5C7, and 6.5D2.

The place and date of recording are included following 6.7B7. Contents are transcribed following 6.7B18. The publisher's number is given in the 028.

Leader   njm   a
Fixed Data 008
  Entrd: nnnnnn Dat tp: s Dates: 1976,   Ctry: ne Comp: pp
  Format: n Audience: Form of item: Accomp mat:
  LitText: n M/E: 1 Lang: eng Mod rec: Source: d

007   sd bumenn

028 02 28 151 XOT $b Island Records

110 20 801 (Musical group)

245 10 801 live $h [sound recording]

260 0   [S.l.] : $b Island Records, $c c1976.

300   1 sound disc : $b analog, 33 1/3 rpm. ; $c 12 in.

518   "Recorded in the Queen Elizabeth Hall, live on the Island Mobile, September 3rd, 1976."

505 0   Lagrima / Manzanera -- TNK / Lennon, McCartney -- East of asteroid / Manzanera, MacCormick -- Rongwrong / Hayward -- Sombre reptiles / Eno -- Baby's on fire / Eno -- Diamond Head / Manzanera -- Miss Shapiro / Manzanera, Eno -- You really got me / Davies -- Third uncle / Eno.

Example 25

CASSETTE PROGRAM

The University of California, Santa Cruz
Board of Studies in Music presents
THE WEDNESDAY EVENING FACULTY RECITAL SERIES

"The Agony and the Irony"

*a lecture/recital
presented in conjunction with Russian Studies
by*

ANATOLE LEIKIN, piano

Performing Arts Concert Hall
February 21, 1990   Wednesday, 8 PM

PROGRAM

Twenty Four Piano Preludes (1933)   **Dmitri Shostakovich**

1. C major, moderato
2. A minor, allegretto
3. G major, andante
4. E minor, moderato
5. D major, allegro vivace
6. B minor, allegretto
7. A major, andante
8. F sharp minor, allegretto
9. E major, presto
10. C sharp minor, moderato
11. B major, allegretto
12. G sharp minor, allegro

13. F sharp major, moderato
14. E flat minor, adagio
15. D flat major, allegretto
16. B flat minor, andantino
17. A flat major, largo
18. F minor, allegretto
19. E flat major, andantino
20. C minor, allegretto furioso
21. B flat major, allegretto
22. G minor, adagio
23. F major, moderato
24. D minor, allegretto

OTHER INFORMATION

The program reproduced above accompanies a locally-produced audio cassette. It is a standard cassette. Written on the box is *ANATOLE LEIKEN recital.* There are also indications that the tape is in stereo and in Dolby B.

SOUND RECORDING WORKFORM

Leader   njm   a
Fixed Data 008
 Entrd: nnnnnn Dat tp: Dates: Ctry: Comp:
 Format: Audience: Form of item: Accomp mat:
 LitText: M/E: Lang: Mod rec: Source:

007

020

028 _ _

047

041 _

1_ _ _ _

245 _ _

260 _

300

4_ _ _ _

5_ _

5_ _

7_ _ _ _

7_ _ _ _

8_ _ _ _

Choice of entry: The choice of main entry begins with 21.13 since this recording is a performance with commentary. The question is whether the commentary or the performance is emphasized. The program, which functions as the chief source of information (6.0B1), is equivocal. It begins by emphasizing the lecture aspect but ends looking like a performance of the preludes. So the last sentence of 21.13D1 was followed, and the tape was entered under a heading appropriate for a performance of the work. Following that leads to 21.23A1, which says to enter a sound recording of a work under the heading appropriate to the work. The form of name was chosen following 22.1A, 22.3A1, 22.4A, 22.5A, and 22.17A (Option). Leikin is given an added entry since he is both performer (21.23A1) and commentator (21.13C1). The form of his name is from the LC Name Authority File, where the form is slightly different from that on the program.

The uniform title was established according to 25.27A, 25.28A, 25.29A1, 25.30A1, 25.30B1, and 25.30C1.

Description: The title is transcribed according to 6.1B1, 6.1C1, 6.1E1 and 6.1F1.

This is not a processed recording; so there is no place of publication or publisher recorded following 6.4C2 and 6.4D4. The date is given following 6.5F3.

The physical description follows 6.5B1, 6.5C2-3, 6.5C6-8, and 6.5D5. Playing speed, number of tracks, and dimensions are omitted because they are standard for the item. The program is described in a note following the LCRI for 1.5E1.

The source of the title is given following 6.7B3. The title of the work being performed is given according to 6.7B4. History of the recording is given following 6.7B7.

Leader   njm   a
Fixed Data 008
  Entrd: nnnnnn Dat tp: s Dates: 1990,   Ctry: xx Comp: pr
  Format: n Audience: Form of item: Accomp mat: z
  LitText: n M/E: 0 Lang: N/A Mod rec: Source: d

007   ss lsnjlc   c

100 10 Shostakovich, Dmitri Dmitrievich, d 1906-1975.

240 10 Preludes, $m piano, $n op. 34

245 14 The agony and the irony $h [sound recording] : $b a lecture/recital presented in conjunction with Russian studies / $c by Anatole Leikin, piano.

260 1 $c 1990.

300   1 sound cassette : $b analog, stereo., Dolby processed

500   Title from program.

500   A performance of Twenty four piano preludes by Shostakovich.

518   Recorded Feb. 21, 1990, in the Performing Arts Concert Hall, University of California, Santa Cruz.

700 10 Leikin, Anatoly, $d 1946-

Example 26

TITLE PAGE

KALMUS PIANO SERIES

Edward
MACDOWELL

WOODLAND SKETCHES

TO A WILD ROSE
WILL O' THE WISP
AT AN OLD TRYSTING PLACE
IN AUTUMN
FROM AN INDIAN LODGE
TO A WATERLILY
FROM UNCLE REMUS
A DESERTED FARM
BY A MEADOW BROOK
TOLD AT SUNSET

EDWIN F. KALMUS
PUBLISHER OF MUSIC
NEW YORK, N.Y.

OTHER INFORMATION

There are 28 pages of music for solo piano; the score is 29.5 cm tall. There is no date of publication.

MUSIC WORKFORM

Leader   ncm   a
Fixed Data 008
  Entrd: nnnnnn Dat tp: Dates: Ctry: Comp:
  Format: Audience: Form of item: Accomp mat:
  LitText: M/E: Lang: Mod rec: Source:

007

020

028 _ _

047

041 _

1__ _ _

245 _ _

260 _

300

4__ _ _

5__

5__

7__ _ _

7__ _ _

8__ _ _

Choice of entry: The choice of main entry is determined by 21.4A1. Choice of name is determined by 22.1A; and form of heading by 22.4A, 22.5A1, and 22.17A (option).

The uniform title is constructed according to 25.27A1.

Description: The title and statement of responsibility are transcribed according to 5.1B1 and 5.1F. 1.1B10 says that, "if the chief source of information bears both a collective title and the titles of individual works, give the collective title as the title proper". Since the individual pieces listed on this title page make up a discrete work, it is not necessary to list the separate pieces in a contents note.

The publication information is transcribed according to 5.4C1, 5.4D1, and 1.4F7. This is a twentieth century publication, but no more exact date can be approximated.

Though a musician might refer to this as a score, the glossary defines a score as "a series of staves on which all the different instrumental and/or vocal parts of a musical work are written." Since this is music for one performer the physical description is done as *p. of music* following 5.5.B1.

The series is transcribed following 5.6B1. The decision to make an added entry for the series was based on 21.30L1 rather than *LCRI* which says to make added entries for all series.

Leader   ncm   a
Fixed Data 008
  Entrd: nnnnnn Dat tp: q Dates: 1900,1990 Ctry: nyu Comp: zz
  Format: z Audience: Form of item: Accomp mat:
  LitText: n M/E: 1 Lang: N/A Mod rec: Source: d

100 10 MacDowell, Edward, $d 1860-1908.

240 10 Woodland sketches

245 10 Woodland sketches /$c Edward MacDowell.

260 0   New York, N.Y. : $b Kalmus, $c [19--]

300   28 p. of music ; $c 30 cm.

490 0   Kalmus piano series

Example 27

TITLE PAGE

Sergei

PROKOFIEV

THE LOVE OF THREE ORANGES
(L'AMOUR DES TROIS ORANGES)

Opus 33

An Opera in Four Acts

for Soli, Chorus and Orchestra
with Russian and French text

VOCAL SCORE

K 05016

Belwin-Mills
Miami, FL

OTHER INFORMATION

There are 252 pages, and the score is 31 cm tall. It includes the vocal parts with French and Russian texts. The accompaniment has been reduced for piano.

There is no date of publication.

MUSIC WORKFORM

Leader   ncm   a
Fixed Data 008
  Entrd: nnnnnn Dat tp: Dates: Ctry: Comp:
  Format: Audience: Form of item: Accomp mat:
  LitText: M/E: Lang: Mod rec: Source:

007

020

028 _ _

047

041 _

1_ _ _ _

245 _ _ _

260 _

300

4_ _ _ _

5_ _

5_ _

7_ _ _ _

7_ _ _ _

8_ _ _ _

Choice of entry: This is a musical work that includes words; so 21.19A1 determines that entry is under the heading for the composer. Choice of name is determined by 22.1A and 22.3C2; form of entry by 22.4A. 22.5A1, and 22.17A (option).

The uniform title is constructed according to 25.27A1, 25.35D1, 25.23F1, and 25.5C, which says to include both languages and to list the original language second.

Description: The title proper is transcribed according to 5.1B1; the parallel title, according to 5.1D1. Other title information follows the part of the title to which it pertains following 1.1E5. The statement of responsibility is transcribed following 5.1F1.

Vocal score is included in the musical presentation area following 5.3B1.

Publication information is transcribed according to 5.4C1, 5.4D1, and 5.4F1. The publisher's number is included in field 028 and coded to produce the note called for in 5.4D3.

The physical description follows 5.5B1 and 5.5D1.

Leader   ncm   a
Fixed Data 008
  Entrd: nnnnnn Dat tp: q Dates: 1900,1990 Ctry: flu Comp: op
  Format: c Audience: Form of item: Accomp mat:
  LitText: n M/E: 1 Lang: rus Mod rec: Source: d

028 30 K 05016 $b Belwin-Mills

041 1   rusfre $h rus

100 10 Prokofiev, Sergey, $d 1891-1953.

240 10 Liubov' k trem apel'sinam. $l French & Russian

245 14 The love of three oranges : $b opus 33 : an opera in four acts for soli, chorus and orchestra with Russian and French text = L'amour des trois oranges / $c Sergei Prokofiev.

254   Vocal score.

260 0   Miami, FL : $b Belwin-Mills, $c [19--]

300   1 vocal score (252 p.) ; $c 31 cm.

740 01 Amour des trois oranges.

Example 28

TITLE PAGE

STRING QUARTET NO. 4

DAVID DIAMOND

For 2 Violins, Viola and 'Cello

Southern Music Publishing Company, Inc. New York

OTHER INFORMATION

The music consists of a score and 4 parts. The title page information comes from the score. The score is 50 pages long and 22.5 cm tall. The parts are 28.5 cm tall. At the bottom of the first page of the score is: copyright 1960

MUSIC WORKFORM

Leader   ncm   a
Fixed Data 008
  Entrd: nnnnnn Dat tp: Dates: Ctry: Comp:
  Format: Audience: Form of item: Accomp mat:
  LitText: M/E: Lang: Mod rec: Source:

007

020

028 _ _

047

041 _

1_ _ _

245 _ _

260 _

300

4_ _ _

5_

5_

7_ _ _

7_ _ _

8_ _ _

Choice of entry: The choice of main entry is determined by 21.1A1. Choice of name is determined by 22.1A; form of heading, by 22.4A, 22.5A1, and 2217A (option).

The uniform title is constructed according to 25.27A1, 25.28A, 25.29A, 25.30A1, 25.30B1, 25.30B3, which says to use *strings* as the medium for this standard combination of instruments, and 25.30C2.

Description: The title proper is transcribed according to 5.1B1. Since the title is the name of a type of composition, the medium and number are considered part of the title proper. There is no other title information. The statement of responsibility is transcribed following 5.1F1.

Publication information is transcribed according to 5.4C1, 5.4D1, and 5.4F1. *Publishing* and *Company* are abbreviated according to Appendix B.9. The physical description follows 5.5B1, 5.5B2, and 5.5D1, which says to give the dimensions of the score and the parts after the detail to which they apply when they differ.

Leader   ncm   a
Fixed Data 008
   Entrd: nnnnnn Dat tp: s Dates: 1960,   Ctry: nyu Comp: zz
   Format: a Audience: Form of item: Accomp mat:
   LitText: n M/E: 1 Lang: N/A Mod rec: Source: d

100 10 Diamond, David, $d 1915-

240 10 Quartets, $m strings, $n no. 4

245 00 String quartet no. 4, for 2 violins, viola and 'cello / $c David Diamond.

260 0   New York : $b Southern Music Pub. Co., $c c1960.

300   1 score (50 p.) ; $c 23 cm. + $a 4 parts ; $c 29 cm.

Example 29

TITLE PAGE

Claude Debussy

LA MER

I. De l'aube a midi sur la mer
II. Jeux de vagues
III. Dialogue du vent et de la mer

Trois Esquisses Symphoniques

A JACQUES DURAND -- 1905

Durand & Cie, Editeurs
Paris, 4, Place de la Madeleine

United Music Publishers Ltd, Londres
Elkan-Vogel Co., Philadelphia, Pa.

Copyright by A. Durand & Fils, 1905, 1909
Copyright by Durand & Cie, 1938

Partition d'orchestre
Partition d'orchestre in-16
Parties d'orchestre
Piano a 2 mains
Piano a 4 mains

OTHER INFORMATION   The score is 135 pages long and 21 cm tall.

MUSIC WORKFORM

Leader   ncm   a
Fixed Data 008
 Entrd: nnnnnn Dat tp: Dates: Ctry: Comp:
 Format: Audience: Form of item: Accomp mat:
 LitText: M/E: Lang: Mod rec: Source:

007

020

028 _ _

047

041 _

1_ _ _

245 _ _

260 _

300

4_ _ _

5_

5_

7_ _ _

7_ _ _

8_ _ _

Choice of entry: The choice of main entry is determined by 21.1A1. Choice of name is determined by 22.1A; form of heading, by 22.4A, 22.5A1, and 22.17A (option).

The uniform title is constructed according to 25.27A1. The initial article is omitted following 25.2C1.

Description: The title proper, other title information, and statement of responsibility are transcribed according to 5.1B1, 5.1E1, and 5.1F1. Following 1.1B10, the titles of the individual parts of the work are not transcribed. Since the titles listed are not for separate works that have been brought together to form a collection but rather for the sections that make up the complete work, it is not necessary to list them in a contents note.

The musical presentation statement is transcribed following 5.3B1. The publication information follows 1.4D5d, which calls for the inclusion of a subsequently named publisher if it is in the home country and the first named is not, 5.4C1 and 5.4D1. The copyright date connected with the current publisher is used according to 1.4F1.

Since the score is reduced in size, *miniature score* is used following 5.5B1. (This is indicated in the 008 format position by *b*.) Dimensions are given following 5.5D1.

Leader   ncm   a
Fixed Data 008
  Entrd: nnnnnn Dat tp: s Dates: 1938,   Ctry: fr Comp: sp
  Format: b Audience: Form of item: a Accomp mat:
  LitText: n M/E: 1 Lang: N/A Mod rec: Source: d

100 10 Debussy, Claude, $ 1862-1918.

240 10 Mer

245 13 La mer : $b trois esquisses symphoniques / $c Claude Debussy.

254   Partition d'orchestre in-16.

260 0   Paris : $b Durand ; $a Philadelphia, Pa. : $b Elkan-Vogel, $c c1938.

300   1 miniature score (135 p.) ; $c 21 cm.

Example 30

TITLE PAGE

TRIO

for Accordion, Trumpet and String Bass

by

Pauline Oliveros

SMITH PUBLICATIONS
American Music

OTHER INFORMATION

There are three identical scores, each is 12 pages long and 32.5 cm tall. There is no title page; the information above comes from the cover. On the first page of music: copyright 1981. Nowhere in the music is there a place of publication.

MUSIC WORKFORM

Leader   ncm   a
Fixed Data 008
 Entrd: nnnnnn Dat tp: Dates: Ctry: Comp:
 Format: Audience: Form of item: Accomp mat:
 LitText: M/E: Lang: Mod rec: Source:

007

020

028 _ _

047

041 _

1_ _ _

245 _ _

260 _

300

4_ _ _

5_

5_

7_ _ _

7_ _ _

8_ _ _

Choice of entry: The choice of main entry is determined by 21.1A1. Choice of name is determined by 22.1A; form of heading, by 22.4A, 22.5A1, and 22.17A (option).

The uniform title is constructed following 25.27A1, 25.28A, 25.29A1, which says to give the name in the plural, 25.30A1, 25.30B1-2, and 25.30B4, which says to use double bass as the name of the instrument listed on the title page as string bass.

Description: The title proper and statement of responsibility are transcribed according to 5.1B1 and 5.1F1. Since the medium is considered part of the title proper, there is no other title information. The publication information is transcribed following 1.4C6, 5.4D1, and 5.4F1. Since the statement *American Music* follows the publisher, the United States is the probable country of publication.

There is a note giving the source of title following 5.7B3.

The physical description is completed according to 5.5B1, 5.5B2, and 5.5D1.

Leader   ncm   a
Fixed Data 008
  Entrd: nnnnnn Dat tp: s Dates: 1981,   Ctry: us Comp: zz
  Format: a Audience: Form of item: Accomp mat:
  LitText: n M/E: 1 Lang: N/A Mod rec: Source: d

100 10 Oliveros, Pauline, $d 1932-

240 10 Trios, $m accordion, trumpet, double bass

245 00 Trio for accordion, trumpet and string bass / $c by Pauline Oliveros.

260 0   [United States] : $b Smith Publications, $c c1981.

300   3 scores (12 p. each) ; $c 33 cm.

500   Cover title.

VISUAL MATERIALS

This USMARC specification is defined for a very wide variety of materials, ranging from original works of art to biological specimens. Any objects not covered in the other specifications will be entered in this one. This specification is also used for describing a kit. The USMARC format defines a kit as "an item that contains a mixture of components from two or more categories, no one of which is the predominant constituent of the item." In the OCLC implementation of this specification, these materials are covered by the *Audiovisual Format*.

AACR2R devotes separate chapters to these materials: Motion pictures and Videorecordings (Chapter 7), Graphic Materials (Chapter 8), and Three-Dimensional Artifacts and Realia (Chapter 10). Kits are dealt with in Rule 1.10, Items Made Up of Several Types of Material. Catalogers should consult the "Scope" section at the beginning of each chapter to determine which chapter is appropriate for which sort of item or object.

The introduction to *AACR2R* recognizes that the rules are not specifically intended for specialist libraries, but should be used as the basis for specialized cataloging and augmented as necessary. Many special libraries that collect heavily in these nonprint media (e.g., slides) may not yet have adopted either *AACR2R* or USMARC as the standards for preparing their catalogs. It is advisable for small general libraries to do so, though, because standardized records can be processed and exchanged more readily than nonstandard records.

Example 31

TITLE FRAME INFORMATION

KEROUAC

Produced and Directed by John Antonelli

written by John Tytel and Frank Cevarich

Narrator   Peter Coyote

With: Allen Ginsberg, Lawrence Ferlinghetti, Michael McClure, William Burroughs, Carolyn Cassady, Herbert Huncke, Joyce Johnson, John Clellon Holmes.

Director of photography: Jerry Jones
Co-producer/editor: Will Parrinello
Music by: Charles Mingus, Duke Ellington, Thelonius Monk, Zoot Sims.

OTHER INFORMATION

The item is a videorecording. Information from outside the item indicates that it was previously released as a motion picture by Jack Kerouac Productions.

On videocassette label: **Color/73 minutes   Docu-Drama**

On cassette container jacket:

Copyright 1985 Active Home Video, Beverly Hills, CA.

This is the award-winning biography of the King of the Beat Generation. Kerouac's life is examined through fascinating rare documentary footage and a masterful portrayal by Jack Coulter. This highly acclaimed film contains revealing interviews with some of Kerouac's most famous contemporaries such as Allen Ginsberg, Lawrence Ferlinghetti and William Burroughs. Beginning with his impoverished Catholic boyhood, through his development as one of the most important modern American authors, to his self-destructive demise at the age of 49, Kerouac is both an accurately detailed documentary and a moving drama.

VHS Hi-Fi SOUND A396

VISUAL MATERIALS WORKFORM

Leader   ngm   a
Fixed Data 008
 Entrd: nnnnnn Dat tp: Dates: ,   Ctry: Leng:
 Audi: Accomp mat: Govt pub: MEBE: Type mat:
 Tech: Lang: Mod rec: Source:

007

1__ _

245 _ _

260

300

5__

5__

5__

7__ __

Choice of entry: The main entry for this work of shared responsibility is the title (21.6C2). The responsibility for the intellectual and artistic contributions to the creation of a theatrical film is always diffuse. Since there are virtually always more than three persons (and usually a production company) involved in the creation of such works, the main entry must be under title.

With so many contributors to such a work, judgment needs to be exercised as to which should have added entries. The LCRI for 21.19 and 21.30 which deals with this judgment. Kerouac receives an author added entry because of the significance of his contribution (some of his poetry readings are filmed). The producer and writers receive added entries because there is no production company openly named.

Description: Chapter 7 is used to describe this item.

The 007 fields contains values that describe the physical medium. The title and statement of responsibility are transcribed from the series of title frames (7.0B1, 7.1B1, 7.1F1). Producers and directors and others considered to be of major importance are recorded in the statement of responsibility (7.1F1 and the LCRI for the rule).

The general material designation (GMD) *videorecording* is transcribed immediately after the title proper (7.1C1). This element is optional. Libraries that follow LC will include this particular GMD (LCRI for 1.1C).

The publication information is recorded per 7.4C, 7.4D, and 7.4F. This data is taken from the cassette label and the cassette container jacket, both of which are prescribed sources, so no bracketing of the information is required (7.0B1, 7.0B2).

The physical description is transcribed per 7.5B1, 7.5C3, 7.5C4, and 7.5D3.

The videorecording system is transcribed in a note (7.7B9f). This note may be recorded as the first note if the cataloger decides it is of primary importance (7.7B).

The narrator and the names of those who appear in the film are recorded in a note if they have not already been recorded in the statement of responsibility (7.7B6). The narrator is recorded in a separate note because the display constant *Narrator:* is to be generated from the machine-readable record. Other contributors not named in the statement of responsibility or in the *Cast* note are recorded in a separate note field (7.7B6). A machine-generated display constant *Credits:* customarily precedes the names and so is not transcribed by the cataloger.

Leader   ngm   a
Fixed Data 008
  Entrd: nnnnnn Dat tp: s Dates: 1985,   Ctry: cau Leng: eng
  Audi: Accomp mat: Govt pub: MEBE: 0 Type mat: v
  Tech: 1   Lang: eng Mod rec: Source: d

007   vf cbaho

245 00 Kerouac $h [videorecording] / $c produced and directed by John Antonelli ; written by John Tytel and Frank Cevarich.

260   Beverly Hills, CA : $b Active Home Video, $c c1985.

300   1 videocassette (73 min.) : $b sd., col. ; $c 1/2 in.

500   VHS format.

511 3 Peter Coyote.

511 1 Jack Coulter, Jack Kerouac, Allen Ginsberg, Lawrence Ferlinghetti, Michael McClure, William Burroughs, Carolyn Cassady, Herbert Huncke, Joyce Johnson, John Clellon Holmes.

508   Director of photography, Jerry Jones; co-producer/editor, Will Parrinello; music, Charles Mingus, Duke Ellington, Theolonius Monk, Zoot Sims.

500   Videocassette release of the motion picture by Jack Kerouac Productions.

520   The life of "Beat Generation" author Jack Kerouac is examined through interviews, documentary film footage, and dramatization.

500   "A 396"

700 11 Kerouac, Jack, $d 1922-1969.

700 11 Antonelli, John.

700 11 Tytel, John.

700 11 Cevarich, Frank.

The data about the previous release as a motion picture is recorded per 7.7B7.

The lengthy and laudatory statement on the cassette container jacket is condensed to a brief objective summary of the content (7.7B17).

The number appearing on the item is recorded in a note per 7.7B19. It is transcribed in quotation marks per 1.7A3.

Example 32

VIDEO TITLE FRAME

DOME CITY

U.C.S.C.

OTHER INFORMATION

Information from outside the item indicates that this videorecording is a reissue of a motion picture originally released in 1969. The video was produced in Santa Cruz, California in 1988. The cataloger timed the length at 8 minutes and determined that the the film has sound and is in color. The videocassette is in VHS format.

In viewing this short videorecording, the cataloger judges that it is about a group of students constructing and living in dome houses on the University of California campus at Santa Cruz.

VISUAL MATERIALS WORKFORM

Leader   ngm   a
Fixed Data 008
 Entrd: nnnnnn Dat tp: Dates: ,   Ctry: Leng:
 Audi: Accomp mat: Govt pub: MEBE: Type mat:
 Tech: Lang: Mod rec: Source:

007

1__ _

245 _ _

260

300

5__

5__

5__

7__ __

Choice of entry: Title main entry is the only possible choice since no individuals or corporate bodies are named as responsible either in the work or elsewhere (21.1C1a).

Description: Chapter 7 is used to describe this item.

The 007 contains values that describe the physical medium. The title is transcribed per 7.0B1a and 7.1B1. The GMD is added in accord with 7.1C1 and the LCRI for that rule.

Publication information is taken from outside the prescribed source, so it must be given in brackets (7.0B2).

The physical description is recorded per 7.5B1, 7.5C3, and 7.5C4.

The videocassette format and history/edition information are recorded in notes prescribed by 7.7B7 and 7.7B10f, respectively. The summary is prescribed in 7.7B18.

Leader   ngm   a
Fixed Data 008
 Entrd: nnnnnn Dat tp: s Dates: 1988,   Ctry: cau Leng: 008
 Audi: Accomp mat: Govt pub: MEBE: 0 Type mat: v
 Tech: 1   Lang: eng Mod rec: Source: d

007   vf cbaho

245 00 Dome City U.C.S.C. $h [videorecording]

260   [Santa Cruz, Calif. : $b s.n., $c 1988]

300   1 videocassette (8 min.) : $b sd., col. ; $c 1/2 in.

500   VHS format.

500   Originally released as a motion picture in 1969.

520   A group of students construct and live in dome houses on the University of California campus at Santa Cruz.

Example 33

DESCRIPTION

This item is a black and white silkscreen print on paper, 67 cm. high and 51 cm. wide, printed on one side only. The subject depicted is a devil on horseback, brandishing a forked spear. The text beneath the figures is a quotation attributed to Thomas Carlyle: *Blessed is he who has found his work*. Following the quotation appears the name: *Thos. Carlyle*. In the lower right-hand corner of the sheet is the printed signature of the graphic artist: *L. C. Davis* and the date *c1971*.

The artist is also known as *L. Clarice Davis*.

VISUAL MATERIALS WORKFORM

Leader   nkm   a
Fixed Data 008
 Entrd: nnnnnn Dat tp: Dates: ,   Ctry: Leng:
 Audi: Accomp mat: Govt pub: MEBE: Type mat:
 Tech: Lang: Mod rec: Source:

007

1__ _

245 _ _

260

300

5__

5__

5__

7__ __

Choice of Entry: This choice may seem straightforward at first, but the work does pose the question of who is chiefly responsible for the intellectual or artistic content. One must consider whether the caption attributed to Carlyle is a text for which the artist has provided the illustration, in which case the main entry would be Carlyle (21.11A1). However, the cataloger has concluded that the artist is chiefly responsible for the entire work because the caption is an integral part of the artwork. The artist is therefore chosen as main entry (21.1A1). An added entry is given for Carlyle as author of the caption. This work might also have been considered as a modification of another work (21.9), in which case the artist would still be chosen for main entry. The work clearly does not qualify as a collaboration between artist and writer (21.24) because they are not contemporaries.

The only form for Davis' name found on the work is *L. C. Davis* so the other forms will not be chosen (21.2A1). The forenames that the initials represent are added to the heading per 22.18.

Description: Chapter 8 is used to describe this item.

The 007 contains values that describe the medium. The title is transcribed per 8.0B1, using the caption text as the title of the artwork. The Library of Congress does not catalog this type of material and so does not specify in its LCRI for 1.1C the use of a GMD. However, the GMD *picture* is listed in 1.1C1 and is appropriate for this item. The statement of responsibility is per 8.1F1. The item is considered published; the existence of the copyright suggests this. Publication data is recorded per 8.4C1, 8.4D1, and 8.4F1.

The physical description is per 8.5B1, 8.5C1b, 8.5C2, and 8.5D1.

The brief summary is required per 8.7B17.

Leader   nkm   a
Fixed Data 008
 Entrd: nnnnnn Dat tp: s Dates: 1971,   Ctry: Leng:
 Audi: Accomp mat: Govt pub: MEBE: 1 Type mat: k
 Tech: n   Lang: eng Mod rec: Source: d

007   kiobo

100 1 Davis, L. C. $q (L. Clarice)

245 10 Blessed is he who has found his work $h [picture] / $c L.C. Davis.

260   [S.l. : $b s.n.], $c c1971.

300   1 art print : $b silkscreen, b&w ; $c 67 x 51 cm.

500   Title from caption.

520   Depicts a devil on horseback brandishing a forked spear, with a caption attributed to Thomas Carlyle.

700 11 Carlyle, Thomas, $d 1795-1881.

Example 34

DESCRIPTION

The material to be cataloged is a collection of 827 black-and-white slides of original photoprints made by the celebrated American photographer Edward Weston between 1920 and 1948. The cataloger has been asked by the slide librarian to make a single MARC-based record for the entire collection, which is known as the "Edward Weston Collection," not to catalog the individual slides. The original photoprints are housed in the Special Collections department of the cataloger's library--in this case, the University of California, Santa Cruz. The slide collection also contains some commercially-produced slides of other Weston photoprints.

The slides, which are 2' x 2', have a safety film emulsion base and are mounted in glass plates secured with plastic tape.

The collection has been classified in the Santa Cruz Slide Classification System.

A computerized catalog, available in the Library's Slide Collection department, provides subject access to records for the individual slides. An appointment is required for viewing the slides, and reproduction of these slides is prohibited by copyright laws.

VISUAL MATERIALS WORKFORM

Leader   n_m   a
Fixed Data 008
 Entrd: nnnnnn Dat tp: Dates: ,   Ctry: Leng:
 Audi: Accomp mat: Govt pub: MEBE: Type mat:
 Tech: Lang: Mod rec: Source:

007

1__ _

245 _ _

260

300

5__

5__

5__

7__ __

Choice of entry: The photographer is the main entry, in accordance with 21.1A2.

Description: Chapter 8 is the principal chapter used to describe this collection. However, since the collection is unique and therefore "archival" in nature, Chapter 4 has also been consulted. This approach is prescribed in the introduction to *AACR2R* (0.23, p. 8): "Use the chapters in part I alone or in combination as the specific problem demands."

Since this collection is archival in nature, the cataloger might consider using the Archival and Manuscript format. However, the Visual Materials format is preferable. The AMC format 007 values pertain only to microforms, whereas the Visual Materials format has 007 values that can be used to describe the physical characteristics of slides. The Visual Materials format also has several variable-length fields that are archival in nature.

The title is transcribed per 8.1B3, and is enclosed in brackets per 8.0B2. Note that if the cataloger follows Elisabeth Betz' *Graphic Materials: Rules for Describing Original Items and Historical Collections* (Washington, D.C.: Library of Congress, 1982), a brief descriptive title may be supplied without brackets (p. 21). The general material designation follows the title proper. This element is optional. Libraries that follow LC will include this particular GMD (LCRI for 1.1C).

This collection is unpublished, therefore no place of publication or name of publisher is recorded (8.4C2, 8.4D2). The inclusive dates of the collection are recorded per 8.4F3.

The physical description is recorded per 8.5B1, 8.5C2. The dimensions of the slides are not given in the description, in accordance with 8.5D5, but the size is coded in the 007 field.

The organization and arrangement of this collection is described per 8.7B10, and entered in field 351. While the description isn't specific, the name of the system mentioned in the note will be recognized by experienced slide users.

The note about the photographer (which the cataloger can construct from information in a biographical dictionary), is the first note given, in accord with 8.7B. The next note is transcribed in accord with 8.7B1 and is combined with data prescribed in 8.7B7. Notes regarding restrictions on use and reproduction of the slides are recorded per 8.7B20, in fields 506 and 540.

The note about access to individual items in the collection via a computerized catalog is prescribed in 4.7B15. The data is entered in field 555, defined for finding aids and cumulative indexes.

Leader   ngm   a

Entrd: nnnnnn   Dat tp: i Dates: 1920,1948 Ctry: Leng: nnn
Audi: Accomp mat: Govt pub: MEBE: 0 Type mat: s
Tech: n   Lang: eng   Mod rec: Source: d

007   gs bj jk

100 1   Weston, Edward, $d 1886-1958.

245 10   [Edward Weston collection] $h [slide]

260      $c [1920-1948]

300   827 slides : $b b&w.

351      $b Classified in the Santa Cruz Slide Classification System.

545   Celebrated American photographer, considered a master of 20th
century photography.

500   The collection consists of slides of the photographer's original photoprints, which were made 1920-1948. The University of California, Santa Cruz also owns the originals, which are housed in the Special Collections department of the University Library. This slide collection also contains some commercially-produced slides of other Weston photoprints.

555 8   A computerized catalog, available in the University Library's Slide Collection, provides subject access to records for the individual slides.

506      $c Appointment required for viewing the slides.

540   Reproduction of these slides is prohibited by copyright laws.

SERIALS

Machine-readable cataloging records are available for most serials being added to library collections. This is mainly due to the CONSER (*CON*version of *SER*ials) Project begun in the 1970s to convert manual serial cataloging into machine-readable records.* While conversion is still an ongoing task, CONSER Project activities now center on current cataloging and data base maintenance, in order to provide authoritative serial records for the cataloging community.

Libraries will inevitably acquire some special and/or local serials that will require original cataloging. Then, too, a serial with an existing record may undergo a change that requires creation of a new record. Your agency may be the first to contribute a new machine-readable record to an online data base, linking the latest title to the record for the previous title.

SERIAL OR MONOGRAPH?

The decision that precedes all others is whether to treat an item as a serial or a monograph. The glossary of *AACR2R* provides the standard definition of a serial:

> . . . a publication in any medium issued in successive parts bearing numeric or chronological designations and intended to be continued indefinitely.

The *Library of Congress rule interpretations* address the treatment for materials in "gray" areas, e.g. college catalogs, conference and exhibition publications, loose-leaf publications, reprints of serials (LCRI for 12.0A). While it is of course possible to catalog a numbered monographic series as a serial, it is now exceedingly rare for the Library of Congress to do so.

LEVEL OF DESCRIPTION

In the examples that follow, the augmented first level description adopted by the Library of Congress will be used (*Cataloging service bulletin* No. 11, Winter 1981). This level produces records somewhere between the first and second levels described in *AACR2R* 1.0D.

* The entire CONSER data base, to which the Library of Congress is a contributor, now resides on the OCLC online system and is also available through tape distribution services and other bibliographic products. Library of Congress serial records will also become available in the near future on CD-ROM.

CHIEF SOURCE OF INFORMATION

A printed serial is described from the title page or title page substitute of the first issue of the serial (12.0B1). If the cataloger does not have the first issue, the serial is described from the first *available* issue, with a note identifying the issue used as the basis for the description (12.7B23). Many serials have no formal title page. *AACR2R* 12.0B1 states the order of preference for the selection of a title page substitute. The title page substitute will frequently be the cover title or, failing that, the caption title. For nonprint serials, the cataloger must also consult other relevant chapters to complete the description (12.0B2).

TRANSCRIBING THE TITLE

The title proper is transcribed exactly as it appears in the chief source of information. This can require frequent exercise of judgment because the presentation of bibliographic data on serials is much less standardized than it is on books. Libraries which follow the *Library of Congress rule interpretations* do not record other title information unless it meets specific conditions (LCRI for 12.1E1). The prescribed sources of information for the remainder of the description of printed serials are treated exceptionally in the LCRI for rule 12.0B1. The cataloger is instructed to use the *whole* publication as the prescribed source of information for the following areas:

> numeric and/or alphabetic, chronological, or other
>   designation area
> publication, distribution, etc., area
> physical description area
> series area

The result of this interpretation is that very little descriptive information will be bracketed in the transcription.

STATEMENT OF RESPONSIBILITY

Editors are not recorded in this area (12.1F3). If considered important to the cataloging agency, they are recorded in a note (12.7B6).

PUBLICATION, DISTRIBUTION, AREA, ETC.

Take care to determine the correct place of publication. Serials will sometimes contain various addresses (editorial, distribution, subscription, etc.). The place becomes particularly significant when it must be used in a uniform title heading to distinguish two different serials with the same title proper. Usually the place of publication (the seat of the editorial function) is given in the serial. When it isn't, the location of the body associated with the copyright statement may be recorded. Some serials carry no explicit information, in which case *s.n.* is recorded (12.4D). Many serials will not carry a publication date. Do not use the chronological designation date (as in, for example, "Vol. 2, Number 4, *May 1990*") for the publication date. Usually a serial will carry a copyright year, which is recorded for the first issue of the serial when no publication date is given. Otherwise, the cataloger with a first issue in hand may supply a bracketed publication date. When the first issue of a serial is not available, no publication date is transcribed.

NOTES

Some of the notes prescribed in 12.7 are input in USMARC fields with special tags. Frequency (12.7B1) is tagged 310 for current frequency and 321 for earlier frequency statements. Variant titles also borne by the serial (12.7B4) and parallel titles (12.7B5) are transcribed in field 246. Notes on serials related to the serial being cataloged (12.7B7) are recorded in *linking entry fields* tagged 76X-78X. The ISSN (12.8B1) is recorded in the 022 field.

CHOICE OF ENTRY

The rules for choice of main entry are the same as those for any type of material and are covered in Chapter 21. Most serials are entered under title because the personal authorship is unknown or diffuse (21.1C1a). Corporate main entry is a possibility, but only when the content of the serial meets the conditions of 21.1B2. Serials of an administrative nature dealing with the corporate body itself (21.B2a) are entered under the heading for the body if more than half of the content is about the body. If, however, more than half of the content is judged to be about other topical subjects, the main entry will be under title.

In accordance with a Library of Congress rule interpretation, a uniform title heading (tag 130) will be added to the description for a serial if it needs to be distinguished from another serial with the same title proper (LCRI for 25.5B1). This is usually the case for titles like *Newsletter, Quarterly, Review, Journal,* etc.

Example 35

TITLE PAGE

The Academy of

Management

REVIEW

VOLUME 13 NUMBER 1 JANUARY 1988 ISSN 0363-7425

OTHER INFORMATION

The verso of the title page provides the following information:

The Academy of Management Review . . . is published by the Academy of Management four times a year in January, April, July and October . . . Business Manager: Walter B. Newsom, P.O. Drawer KZ, Mississippi State University, MS 39762-5865.

There are no illustrations and the size is 24 cm.

There is no place given for the editorial function.

According to *New Serial Titles*, 1976, this serial began in January 1976, superseding a serial called Academy of Management journal. That serial had ISSN 0001-4273.

SERIAL WORKFORM

Leader   nas   a_
Fixed Data 008
  Entrd: nnnnnn Pub st: Dates: -   Ctry:
  Frequn: Regulr: ISDS: Ser tp:
  Form of orig item: Form of item: Nature of work:
  Nature of cont: Govt pub: Conf pub: Titl pag:
  Indx: Cum ind: Alphabt: S/L ent: Lang:
  Mod rec: Source:

1__ _ _

245 _ _

246 _ _

260 0 0

300

310

362 _

5__

5__

7__ __

7__ __

Choice of entry: Examination of the serial reveals that the articles are not about the Academy of Management, so corporate body main entry is not appropriate. The main entry is under title (21.1C1c), with an added entry for the corporate body (21.30E). The form of the added entry follows 24.1A.

Description: The ISSN is recorded (12.8B1). The title is transcribed according to 12.1B1 and 12.1B3.

The publication data is recorded per 12.4C1 and 12.4D1. The publisher's name is given in a shortened form (1.4D4). Since the first issue published is not available to the cataloger, no date is recorded. The physical description is per 12.5B1 and 12.5D1. The frequency is prescribed in 12.7B1.

The data in the 362 field is recorded per 12.3C4. It is input with first indicator value *1* to signify unformatted style. This style of note is used when the first and/or last issue is not in hand, but the information is known. The cataloger must base the rest of the description, however, on the first *available* issue.

When the first issue is not available, a note (500 field) identifies the issue on which the description is based (12.7B23). When the source of the title proper is other than the chief source of information, that source is recorded in a note (12.7B3). The note is combined with the note identifying the issue on which the description is based.

The previous title is recorded in a note (12.7B7b). It is input in a linking entry field (780) without the word *Continues*, because implementations of USMARC are expected to generate the word as a display/print constant. The format provides for recording the ISSN in subfield *x* of the linking entry field. Leader position 19 contains the value *r* to indicate the requirement for a related record.

Leader   nas   ar
Fixed Data 008
  Entrd: nnnnnn Pub st: c Dates: 1976-9999 Ctry: msu
  Frequn: q Regulr: r ISDS: Ser tp: p
  Form of orig item: Form of item: Nature of work:
  Nature of cont: Govt pub: Conf pub: 0 Titl pag: u
  Indx: u Cum ind: u Alphabt: a S/L ent: 0 Lang: eng
  Mod rec: Source: d

022   0363-7425

245 04 The Academy of Management review.

260 00 Mississippi State, MS : $b The Academy,

300   v. ; $c 24 cm.

310   Quarterly

362 1   Began with Jan. 1976 issue.

500   Description based on: Vol. 13, no. 1 (Jan. 1988); title from cover.

710 20 Academy of Management.

780 00 $t Academy of Management journal $x 0001-4273

Example 36

TITLE PAGE

ADVANCES IN THE ECONOMIC ANALYSIS OF PARTICIPATORY AND LABOR-MANAGED FIRMS

A Research Annual

EDITORS:

DEREK C. JONES
Department of Economics
Hamilton College

JAN SVEJNAR
Department of Economics
Cornell University

VOLUME 1 - 1985

JAI PRESS INC.

Greenwich, Connecticut   London, England

OTHER INFORMATION

The verso of title page includes the following information: **Copyright 1985. ISBN: 0-89232-583-6.**

There are no illustrations and the size is 26 cm.

SERIAL WORKFORM

Leader   nas   a_
Fixed Data 008
 Entrd: nnnnnn Pub st: Dates: -   Ctry:
 Frequn: Regulr: ISDS: Ser tp:
 Form of orig item: Form of item: Nature of work:
 Nature of cont: Govt pub: Conf pub: Titl pag:
 Indx: Cum ind: Alphabt: S/L ent: Lang:
 Mod rec: Source:

1_ _ _

245 _ _

246 _ _

260 0 0

300

310

362 _

5_

5_

7_ _

7_ _

Choice of entry: This serial is produced under editorial direction by editors named prominently. The rule that applies for choice of main entry is 21.7B1, which says to enter such works under title and make added entries for the prominently named editors if there are not more than three. Rule 21.30D1 says to make an added entry for an editor of a serial only if it is likely to be known by the editor's name. In this example, the work may very well be searched for under the editors. The forms of the headings for the editors are established under 22.1B and 22.5A1.

Description: The title is transcribed following 12.1B1. Other title information (*A Research Annual*) is not recorded in the 245 field (LCRI for 12.1E1). An editor is not recorded in the statement of responsibility (12.1F3). If an editor statement is considered necessary by a cataloging agency, it is given in a note with tag 570.

Only the first place of publication and the associated publisher are recorded. This follows the augmented first level description that LC has adopted for serials. The date in recorded per 12.4F1.

The physical description is per 12.5B1 and 12.5D1. The frequency is transcribed per 12.7B1. The data in the 362 field is recorded per 12.3C4. The editor statement is prescribed in 12.7B6.

There is no provision either in *AACR2R* or USMARC for recording an ISBN (International Standard *Book* Number) in a serial record.

Leader   nas   a
Fixed Data 008
  Entrd: nnnnnn Pub st: c Dates: 1985-9999 Ctry: ctu
  Frequn: a   Regulr: r ISDS: Ser tp:
  Form of orig item: Form of item: Nature of work:
  Nature of cont: Govt pub: Conf pub: 0 Titl pag: u
  Indx: u Cum ind: u Alphabt: a S/L ent: 0 Lang: eng
  Mod rec: Source: d

245 00 Advances in the economic analysis of participatory and
            labor-managed firms.

260 00 Greenwich, Conn. : $b JAI Press, $c c1985-

300   v. ; $c 26 cm.

310   Annual

362 0   Vol. 1 (1985)-

570   Editors: 1985-   D.C. Jones and J. Svejnar.

700 10 Jones, Derek C.

700 10 Svejnar, Jan.

Example 37

TITLE PAGE

APPLIED PHYSICS B

PHOTOPHYSICS AND LASER CHEMISTRY

Volume B 26   Number 1   September 1981

Springer-Verlag   Berlin   Heidelberg   New York

ISSN 0340-3793   (Published monthly)   September 1981

OTHER INFORMATION

The data above appears on the cover of the issue. There is no title page. This is the first issue with this title.

The issues are illustrated and the size is 28 cm.

The serial *Applied Physics* split into several separate serials in 1981. This serial is one of those resulting from the split.

SERIAL WORKFORM

Leader   nas   a_
Fixed Data 008
  Entrd: nnnnnn Pub st: Dates: -   Ctry:
  Frequn: Regulr: ISDS: Ser tp:
  Form of orig item: Form of item: Nature of work:
  Nature of cont: Govt pub: Conf pub: Titl pag:
  Indx: Cum ind: Alphabt: S/L ent: Lang:
  Mod rec: Source:

1 _ _ _

245 _ _

246 _ _

260 0 0

300

310

362 _

5 _

5 _

7 _ _

7 _ _

Choice of entry: The main entry is under title in accordance with 21.1C1a. The added entry for the title of section *B*, input in the 246 field, is made per 21.30J1.

Description: The ISSN is recorded (2.8B1) The title is transcribed according to 12.1B4.

The publication data follows 12.4C1, 1.4C5, 12.4D1, and 12.4F1. The physical description is per 12.5B1, 12.5C1, and 12.5D1, and the frequency is per 12.7B1. The data in field 362 is recorded per 12.3C4. The source of the title proper is recorded per 12.7B3.

The relationship of this new serial to the previous serial that split into parts is stated in a note (12.7B7e). This serial continues in part the earlier serial. The uniform title heading for the previous serial is entered in a linking entry field (tag 780). The relationship *Continues in part* is expressed through the second indicator digit *1*. Leader position 19 contains the value *r* to indicate the requirement for a related record.

Leader   nas   ar
Fixed Data 008
 Entrd: nnnnnn Pub st: c   Dates: 1981-9999 Ctry: wb
 Frequn: m   Regulr: r ISDS: Ser tp: p
 Form of orig item: Form of item: Nature of work:
 Nature of cont: Govt pub: Conf pub: 0 Titl pag: u
 Indx: u Cum ind: u Alphabt: a   S/L ent: 0 Lang: eng
 Mod rec: Source: d

022   0340-3793

245 00 Applied physics. $n B, $p Photophysics and laser chemistry.

246 30 Photophysics and laser chemistry

260 00 Berlin ; $a New York : $b Springer-Verlag, $c 1981-

300   v. : $b ill. ; $c 28 cm.

310   Monthly

362 0   Vol. B26, no. 1 (Sept. 1981)-

500   Title from cover.

780 01 $t Applied physics

Example 38

TITLE PAGE

National Endowment
for the Arts

Volume 4, No. 2
Winter 1987

ARTS

R E V I E W

OTHER INFORMATION

ISSN: 0741-4579.

Published in Washington, D.C. by the National Endowment for the Arts.

There are illustrations and the size is 30 cm.

There is another serial with the same title proper.

Issues for Vol. 4, no. 3 (spring 1987)- have title: Artsreview.

SERIAL WORKFORM

Leader   nas   a_
Fixed Data 008
 Entrd: nnnnnn Pub st: Dates: -   Ctry:
 Frequn: Regulr: ISDS: Ser tp:
 Form of orig item: Form of item: Nature of work:
 Nature of cont: Govt pub: Conf pub: Titl pag:
 Indx: Cum ind: Alphabt: S/L ent: Lang:
 Mod rec: Source:

1_ _ _

245 _ _

246 _ _

260 0 0

300

310

362 _

5_

5_

7_ _

7_ _

Choice of entry: The main entry is under title (21.1C1c). Because there is a different serial with the same title proper, a uniform title heading (tag 130), composed of the title proper plus an explanatory designation in parentheses, is required (25.5B and the LCRI for this rule).

Description: The ISSN is recorded (12.8B1). The title and statement of responsibility are recorded following 12.1B1 and 12.1F1. The publication data is recorded per 12.4C1 and 12.4D1. No date is recorded since the first issue is not available. The physical description is according to 12.5B1, 12.5C1, and 12.5D1. The frequency is per 12.7B1. A note cites the item on which the description is based (12.7B23), and the source of the title proper is included in the note (12.7B3).

Presentation of the title from spring 1987 forward as one word rather than two words does not constitute a title change, so the variant form is recorded in a 246 field and a note describes when the change occurred (21.2A and the LCRI for this rule).

Leader   nas   a
Fixed Data 008
 Entrd: nnnnnn Pub st: c   Dates: 19uu-9999 Ctry: dcu
 Frequn: q   Regulr: r ISDS: Ser tp: p
 Form of orig item: Form of item: Nature of work:
 Nature of cont: Govt pub: Conf pub: 0 Titl pag: u
 Indx: u Cum ind: u Alphabt: a S/L ent: 0 Lang: eng
 Mod rec: Source: d

022   0741-4579

130 00 Arts review (Washington, D.C.)

245 00 Arts review / $c National Endowment for the Arts.

246 13 Artsreview

260 0 Washington, D.C. : $b National Endowment for the Arts,

300   v. : $b ill. ; $c 30 cm.

310   Quarterly

500   Vol. 4, no. 3 (spring 1987)-   have title: Artsreview.

500   Description based on: Vol. 4, no. 2 (winter 1987); title from
        cover.

Example 39

TITLE PAGE

March 1990

vol. 13 no. 1

CARL Newsletter

California Academic & Research Librarians

OTHER INFORMATION

The last page of the newsletter says: **The CARL Newsletter is the official newsletter of the California Academic and Research Librarians association. It is published quarterly . . . Lee Jaffe, Editor . . . Santa Cruz, Calif.**

The title appears at the head of page 1 of the text. There is no title page or cover.

There are no illustrations and the size is 28 cm.

Articles are predominantly on the association, its activities, and its members.

SERIAL WORKFORM

Leader   nas   a_
Fixed Data 008
  Entrd: nnnnnn Pub st: Dates: -   Ctry:
  Frequn: Regulr: ISDS: Ser tp:
  Form of orig item: Form of item: Nature of work:
  Nature of cont: Govt pub: Conf pub: Titl pag:
  Indx: Cum ind: Alphabt: S/L ent: Lang:
  Mod rec: Source:

1_ _ _

245 _ _

246 _ _

260 0 0

300

310

362 _

5_

5_

7_ _

7_ _

Choice of entry: The main entry is under the corporate body because examination of the issues reveals that the predominant content is information about the organization and its activities (21.1B2a and the LCRI for this rule). The form of heading for the body was found in the LC Names Authority File, and is based on 24.2.

Description: The title and statement of responsibility are transcribed per 12.1B1 and 12.1F1. The location of the editor is assumed to be the place of publication. The publisher is supplied by the cataloger per 12.4D1 and is bracketed because it is not taken from the prescribed source for such information. The acronym is used for the supplied publisher per 1.4D4. The physical description is per 12.5B1 and 12.5D1. The frequency is per 12.7B1. The note regarding the source of the title proper (12.7B3) is combined with the note citing the item on which the description is based (12.7B23).

Leader   nas   a
Fixed Data 008
  Entrd: nnnnnn Pub st: c   Dates: 19uu-9999 Ctry: cau
  Frequn: q   Regulr: r ISDS: Ser tp: p
  Form of orig item: Form of item: Nature of work:
  Nature of cont: Govt pub: Conf pub: 0 Titl pag: u
  Indx: u Cum ind: u Alphabt: a S/L ent: 0 Lang: eng
  Mod rec: Source: d

110 20 California Academic and Research Librarians.

245 10 CARL newsletter / $c California Academic & Research Librarians.

260 00 Santa Cruz, Calif. : $b [CARL],

300   v. ; $c 28 cm.

310   Quarterly

500   Description based on: Vol. 13, no. 1 (Mar. 1990); title from
         caption.

Example 40

TITLE PAGE

CAT FANCY

The Magazine for Responsible Cat Owners

January 1986

Volume 29, Number 1

OTHER INFORMATION

The masthead of the magazine says:

> Cat Fancy (ISSN 0892-6514) is published monthly
> Published by Fancy Publications Inc. . . . San Juan Capistrano, Calif.
>
> Corporate headquarters at 2401 Beverly Blvd.,
> Los Angeles, CA 90057-0900
> Subscription Dept. . . . Boulder, CO 80322

This is the **microfilm reproduction** of the printed serial. The title appears on the cover; there is no title page. The microfilm edition is being produced by Micro Photo Inc., Cleveland, Ohio, beginning in 1987. The film is 35 mm., positive image, normal reduction, silver halide, safety base film.

The issues contain color illustrations. The size of the printed version is not known.

This serial began in 1966 with the title *Cat Fancy*. From the mid-1980s until the end of 1985, the title was *International Cat Fancy*, then it changed back to *Cat Fancy*. In January 1988, the place of publication changed to Irvine, California.

SERIAL WORKFORM

Leader   nas   a_
Fixed Data 008
 Entrd: nnnnnn Pub st: Dates: -   Ctry:
 Frequn: Regulr: ISDS: Ser tp:
 Form of orig item: Form of item: Nature of work:
 Nature of cont: Govt pub: Conf pub: Titl pag:
 Indx: Cum ind: Alphabt: S/L ent: Lang:
 Mod rec: Source:

1_ _ _

245 _ _

246 _ _

260 0 0

300

310

362 _

5__

5__

7__ __

7__ __

Choice of entry: The main entry is under title in accordance with 21.1C1c. Since this serial changed its title in 1986 to the same title it had originally in 1966, a uniform title heading (tag 130) is needed to distinguish the record for this serial from the record for the earlier one (25.5B and the LCRI for that rule).

Description: The standard practice for describing microform reproductions is that of the Library of Congress. LC does not follow *AACR2R* but instead describes the original work in all areas except the note area, then describes the reproduction in the note area (LCRI for Chapter 11).

The 007 field contains values that describe the microfilm medium. The ISSN is recorded (12.8B1). The title is transcribed per 12.1B1. The GMD is added after the title, per 12.1C1. The publication data is transcribed following 12.4C1, 12.4D1, and 12.4F1. The physical description is per 12.5B1 and 12.5C1. The frequency is recorded per 12.7B1, and the data is the 362 field is recorded per 12.3C4. The source of the title proper is given per 12.7B3.

When the place of publication used in a uniform title heading changes, the heading in the record remains the same (LCRI for 21.3B1). A note is added to describe the new place of publication (12.7B9). The bibliographic data describing the reproduction is recorded in field 533.

The note about the previous title, which is prescribed in 12.7B7b, is recorded in a 780 linking entry field without the word *Continues*, which is generated in displays by means of the indicator digits. Position 19 in the Leader contains value *r* to reflect the presence of this field.

Leader   nas   ar
Fixed Data 008
  Entrd: nnnnnn Pub st: c Dates: 1986-9999 Ctry: cau
  Frequn: m Regulr: r ISDS: Ser tp: p
  Form of orig item: Form of item: a Nature of work:
  Nature of cont: Govt pub: Conf pub: 0 Titl pag: u
  Indx: u Cum ind: u Alphabt: a S/L ent: 0 Lang: eng
  Mod rec: Source: d

007   hdrafu---caua

022   0892-6514

130 00 Cat fancy (San Juan Capistrano, Calif.)

245 00 Cat fancy $h [microfilm]

260 00 San Juan Capistrano, Calif. : $b Fancy Publications, $c c1986-

300   v. : $b ill. ; $c

310   Monthly

362 0   Vol. 29, no. 1 (Jan. 1986)-

500   Title from cover.

500   Published in Irvine, Calif., Jan. 1988-

533   Microfilm. $b Cleveland, Ohio : $c Micro Photo Inc., $d 1987- $e   microfilm reels ;
35 mm.

780 00 $t International cat fancy

Example 41

TITLE PAGE

THE DUDLEY KNOX LIBRARY

PERIODICAL HOLDINGS

Annual alphabetical listing

January 1988

OTHER INFORMATION

A circular logo on the title page includes the following: DEPART-MENT OF THE NAVY NAVAL POSTGRADUATE SCHOOL MONTEREY, CALIFORNIA

The information above appears on the cover and there is no title page.

There are no illustrations and the size is 28 cm.

SERIAL WORKFORM

Leader   nas   a_
Fixed Data 008
  Entrd: nnnnnn Pub st: Dates: -   Ctry:
  Frequn: Regulr: ISDS: Ser tp:
  Form of orig item: Form of item: Nature of work:
  Nature of cont: Govt pub: Conf pub: Titl pag:
  Indx: Cum ind: Alphabt: S/L ent: Lang:
  Mod rec: Source:

1_ _ _

245 _ _

246 _ _

260 0 0

300

310

362 _

5_

5_

7_ _

7_ _

Choice of entry: The main entry is under the corporate body (21.1B2a). The form of the heading for the body is according to 24.17A. The name of the library does not fall under any of the types of names listed in 24.18 that are entered subordinately.

Description: The title is recorded per 12.1B1. The statement of responsibility is transcribed per 12.1F1. It precedes the title in the chief source of information and is transposed per 1.1F3. Other title information is not recorded in the 245 (LCRI for 12.1E1). The publication information is recorded per 12.4C1 and 12.4D1, with the publisher's name supplied by the cataloger in an abbreviated form per 1.4D4. The frequency is transcribed per 12.7B1. The note on the source of the title is combined with the note citing the item on which the description is based (12.7B3, 12.7B23).

Leader   nas   a
Fixed Data 008
  Entrd: nnnnnn Pub st: c Dates: 19uu-9999 Ctry: cau
  Frequn: a Regulr: r ISDS: Ser tp:
  Form of orig item: Form of item: Nature of work:
  Nature of cont: Govt pub: f Conf pub: 0 Titl pag: u
  Indx: u Cum ind: u Alphabt: a S/L ent: 0 Lang: eng
  Mod rec: Source: d

110 20 Dudley Knox Library.

245 10 Periodical holdings / $c The Dudley Knox Library, Department of the Navy, Naval
Postgraduate School.

260 00 Monterey, Calif. : $b [The Library,

300   v. ; $c 28 cm.

310   Annual

500   Description based on: Jan. 1988; title from cover.

Example 42

TITLE PAGE

THE INTERCOLLEGIATE REVIEW

A Journal of Scholarship and Opinion

Vol. 25 No. 2   Spring 1990

OTHER INFORMATION

The masthead of the journal includes the following information:

Published 2-4 times during the academic year
by the Intercollegiate Studies Institute, Inc.
14 South Bryn Mawr Avenue
Bryn Mawr, Pennsylvania
0020-5249

The title appears on the cover and there is no title page.

The issues have no illustrations and the size is 26 cm.

SERIAL WORKFORM

Leader   nas   a_
Fixed Data 008
  Entrd: nnnnnn Pub st: Dates: -   Ctry:
  Frequn: Regulr: ISDS: Ser tp:
  Form of orig item: Form of item: Nature of work:
  Nature of cont: Govt pub: Conf pub: Titl pag:
  Indx: Cum ind: Alphabt: S/L ent: Lang:
  Mod rec: Source:

1__ _ _

245 _ _

246 _ _

260 0 0

300

310

362 _

5__

5__

7__ __

7__ __

Choice of entry: The main entry is under title because examination of the issues reveals that the articles are not about the Institute (21.1C1c). An added entry is made for the Institute per 21.30E. The form of the heading is per 24.1A.

Description: The ISSN is recorded (12.8B1). The title is transcribed according to 12.1B1. Other title information is not recorded (LCRI for 12.1E1). The publication data is transcribed per 12.4C1 and 12.4C2. No date is recorded since this is not the first issue. The frequency is recorded in the 310 field as it appears (12.7B1), except that the initial numerals in a note must be spelled out (Appendix C.4A). Note the coding for *Frequn* and *Regulr* in the fixed field. The note about the source of the title proper (12.7B3) is combined with the note about the item on which the description is based (12.7B23).

Leader   nas   a
Fixed Data 008
  Entrd: nnnnnn Pub st: c Dates: 19uu-9999 Ctry: pau
  Frequn: q Regulr: r ISDS: Ser tp: p
  Form of orig item: Form of item: Nature of work:
  Nature of cont: Govt pub: Conf pub: 0 Titl pag: u
  Indx: u Cum ind: u Alphabt: a S/L ent: 0 Lang: eng
  Mod rec: Source: d

022   0020-5249

245 04 The Intercollegiate review.

260 00 Bryn Mawr, Penn. : $b Intercollegiate Studies Institute,

300   v. ; $c 26 cm.

310   Two-four times during the academic year

500   Description based on: Vol. 25, no. 2 (spring 1990); title
      from cover.

710 20 Intercollegiate Studies Institute.

Example 43

TITLE PAGE

NEWSLETTER

ACLS

Volume 1, No. 1 (second series), Summer 1987

OTHER INFORMATION

The second page of the newsletter includes the following information: **American Council of Learned Societies ... New York, NY ... The Newsletter of the Council is published four times a year.**

The title appears at the head of page 1 of the text.

There are illustrations and the size is 28 cm.

Less than half of an issue is devoted to the Council itself.

This first issue continues the Council's publication called *ACLS Newsletter*, which was devoted predominantly to the activities of the Council and was cataloged with the Council as the main entry.

SERIAL WORKFORM

Leader   nas   a_
Fixed Data 008
  Entrd: nnnnnn Pub st: Dates: -   Ctry:
  Frequn: Regulr: ISDS: Ser tp:
  Form of orig item: Form of item: Nature of work:
  Nature of cont: Govt pub: Conf pub: Titl pag:
  Indx: Cum ind: Alphabt: S/L ent: Lang:
  Mod rec: Source:

1_ _ _

245 _ _

246 _ _

260 0 0

300

310

362 _

5_

5_

7_ __

7_ __

Choice of entry: The main entry is under title because the issues are not predominantly devoted to the Council (21.1C1c). A uniform title heading (tag 130) is required to distinguish this serial from numerous other serials with the same title proper (25.5B and the LCRI for the rule). An added entry is made for the Council per 21.30E. The form for the heading is per 24.1A.

Description: The title and statement of responsibility are transcribed per 12.1B1 and 12.1F1. The publication data is recorded per 12.4C1, 12.4D1, and 12.4F1. The physical description is per 12.5B1, 12.5C1, and 12.5D1. The frequency is transcribed per 12.7B1. The data in the 362 field is recorded per 12.3C4, using abbreviations and numerals as specified in Appendices B and C. The source of the title proper is transcribed per 12.7B3. The note regarding the previous title is required by 12.7B7b. It is input in a linking entry field (780) in the form in which it was cataloged (author/title entry). The relationship statement *Continues* will be generated in displays by means of the indicator digits. Leader position 19 contains the value *r* to reflect the requirement for a related record.

Leader   nas   ar
Fixed Data 008
  Entrd: nnnnnn Pub st: c   dates: 1987-9999   Ctry: nyu
  Frequn: q   Regulr: r   ISDS: Ser tp: p
  Form of orig item: Form of item: Nature of work:
  Nature of cont: Govt pub: Conf pub: 0   Titl pag: u
  Indx: u Cum ind: u   Alphabt: a S/L ent: 0 Lang: eng
  Mod rec: Source: d

130 00 Newsletter (American Council of Learned Societies)

245 00 Newsletter / $c ACLS.

260 00 New York, NY : $b American Council of Learned Societies, $c [1987-

300   v. : $b ill. ; $c 28 cm.

310   Quarterly

362 0   2nd ser., v. 1, no. 1 (summer 1987)-

500   Title from caption.

710 20 American Council of Learned Societies.

780 00 American Council of Learned Societies. $t ACLS newsletter

Example 44

TITLE PAGE

RESPONSE

A CONTEMPORARY JEWISH REVIEW

OTHER INFORMATION

The title is from the cover and there is no title page.

On verso of cover: **RESPONSE (ISSN: 0034-5709) is published quarterly: Fall, Winter, Spring, and Summer by Response Magazine, Inc. . . . Editorial Office . . . New York, NY.**

The issues are illustrated and the size is 23 cm.

On Table of Contents page: Vol. XV, No. 4 Fall 1987.

It is known that the serial began with the summer 1967 issue.

There is another serial with the same title proper, published in the same city.

SERIAL WORKFORM

Leader   nas   a_
Fixed Data 008
 Entrd: nnnnnn Pub st: Dates: -   Ctry:
 Frequn: Regulr: ISDS: Ser tp:
 Form of orig item: Form of item: Nature of work:
 Nature of cont: Govt pub: Conf pub: Titl pag:
 Indx: Cum ind: Alphabt: S/L ent: Lang:
 Mod rec: Source:

1__ __ __

245 __ __

246 __ __

260 0 0

300

310

362 _

5__

5__

7__ __

7__ __

Choice of entry: The main entry is under title (21.1C1a). A uniform title heading is added to distinguish this serial from the other serial with the same title. In constructing this uniform title heading, the first year of publication is added to the place of publication since both serials are published in New York (25.5B1 and the LCRI for this rule).

Description: The ISSN is recorded (12.8B1). The title proper is transcribed according to 12.1B1. Other title information is not recorded (LCRI for 12.1E1). The publication data is per 12.4C1 and 12.4D1. The physical description follows 12.5B1, 12.5C1, and 12.5D1. The frequency is recorded per 12.7B1. The known information about the first issue published is transcribed per 12.3B1 and recorded in an unformatted 362 field (first indicator digit *1*).

The note for the source of the title proper (12.7B3) is combined with the note citing the item on which the description is based (12.7B23).

Leader   nas   a
Fixed Data 008
  Entrd: nnnnnn Pub st: c Dates: 1967-9999 Ctry: nyu
  Frequn: q Regulr: r ISDS: Ser tp: p
  Form of orig item: Form of item: Nature of work:
  Nature of cont: Govt pub: Conf pub: 0 Titl pag: u
  Indx: u Cum ind: u Alphabt: a S/L ent: 0 Lang: eng
  Mod rec: Source: d

022   0034-5709

130 00 Response (New York, N.Y. : 1967)

245 00 Response.

260 00 New York, N.Y. : $b Response,

300   v. : $b ill. ; $c 23 cm.

310   Quarterly

362 1   Began with summer 1967 issue.

500   Description based on: Vol. 15, no. 4 (fall 1987); title
     from cover.

Example 45

TITLE PAGE

Response To the Victimization of Women and Children

JOURNAL OF THE CENTER FOR WOMEN POLICY STUDIES

Volume 10   Number 3   1987

OTHER INFORMATION

ISSN: 0894-7597.

Began with Vol. 7, no. 4, fall 1984.

From fall 1984-198 , published by the Center, in Washington, D.C.

Size is 28 cm. and there are no illustrations.

Published quarterly.

Continues: Response to violence in the family & sexual assault, ISSN 0737-8300.

SERIAL WORKFORM

Leader   nas   a_
Fixed Data 008
  Entrd: nnnnnn Pub st: Dates: -   Ctry:
  Frequn: Regulr: ISDS: Ser tp:
  Form of orig item: Form of item: Nature of work:
  Nature of cont: Govt pub: Conf pub: Titl pag:
  Indx: Cum ind: Alphabt: S/L ent: Lang:
  Mod rec: Source:

1__ _ _

245 _ _

246 _ _

260 0 0

300

310

362 _

5__

5__

7__ __

7__ __

Choice of entry: The main entry is under title (21.1C1c). Examination of the issues reveals that the articles are not about the Center, so corporate main entry under 21.1B2 is not appropriate. The added entry for the Center is made in accordance with 21.30E1. The form of the heading is per 24.1A.

Description: The ISSN is recorded (12.8B1). The title proper is transcribed per 12.1B1. Rule 12.1E1 is followed in this case, and other title information *is* recorded. The LCRI for this rule states that other title information will be recorded when it includes a statement of responsibility that is embedded in the other title information.

The publication data is recorded per 12.4C1 and 12.4D1. Authoritative information about the publication of the first issue may be recorded in the 260 field. Then, publication information about the first *available* issue is recorded in a note (12.7B9). The cataloger must be careful not to assume too much about a first issue that is not in hand. When any data is in doubt, it should not be entered in a shared data base. CONSER participants will supply authoritative data later, if and when they enhance the record.)

The frequency is recorded (12.7B1).

The known information about the first issue published is transcribed per 12.3B1 and recorded in an unformatted 362 field (first indicator digit *1*).

The note for the source of the title proper (12.7B3) is combined with the note citing the item on which the description is based (12.7B23).

The note regarding the earlier title is prescribed in 12.7B7b. It is recorded in a 780 field, which accommodates the *Continues* relationship by means of indicator digits, and provides for entry of the ISSN in subfield *x*. Leader position 19 contains the value *r* to signify the requirement for a related record.

Leader   nas   ar
Fixed Data 008
  Entrd: nnnnnn Pub st: c Dates: 1984-9999 Ctry: dcu
  Frequn: q   Regulr: r ISDS: Ser tp: p
  Form of orig item: Form of item: Nature of work:
  Nature of cont: Govt pub: Conf pub: 0 Titl pag: u
  Indx: u   Cum ind: u   Alphabt: a S/L ent: 0 Lang: eng
  Mod rec: Source: d

022   0894-7597

245 00 Response to the victimization of women and children : $b
        journal of the Center for Women Policy Studies.

260 00 Washington, D.C. : $b The Center,

300   v. ; $c 28 cm.

310   Quarterly

361 1   Began with Vol. 7, no. 4, fall 1984.

500   Published: New York, N.Y. : Guilford Press, 198 -

500   Description based on Vol. 10, no. 3 (1987); title from
        cover.

710 20 Center for Women Policy Studies.

780 00 $t Response to violence in the family & sexual assault
        $x 0737-8300

Example 46

TITLE PAGE

VALLEY PRESS

Serving the San Lorenzo Valley

Vol. XXX, No. 27 Wednesday, June 6, 1990

OTHER INFORMATION

The masthead includes the following information:

> Postal Service Publication No. 906-620
> The Valley Press is published weekly each Wednesday.
> Offices are located at . . . Felton, CA
> Member of the California Newspaper Publishers Association

The title appears at the head of page 1 of the text.

There are several other serial publications with the same title proper.

The size is 48 cm. and there are illustrations.

SERIAL WORKFORM

Leader   nas   a_
Fixed Data 008
 Entrd: nnnnnn Pub st: Dates: - Ctry:
 Frequn: Regulr: ISDS: Ser tp:
 Form of orig item: Form of item: Nature of work:
 Nature of cont: Govt pub: Conf pub: Titl pag:
 Indx: Cum ind: Alphabt: S/L ent: Lang:
 Mod rec: Source:

1__ __ __

245 __ __

246 __ __

260 0 0

300

310

362 __

5__

5__

7__ __

7__ __

Choice of entry: The main entry is under title (21.1C1a). A uniform title heading is added to distinguish this serial from the other serials with the same title (25.5B1 and the LCRI for this rule).

Description: The U.S. Postal Service number is recorded (12.7B19, 12.8B2) in the appropriate USMARC field. The title proper is transcribed per 12.1B1. The publication data is recorded per 12.4C1 and 12.4D1. The physical description follows 12.5B1, 12.5C1, and 12.5D1. The frequency is recorded (12.7B1).

The information recorded in the 520 field helps identify the scope of this serial and the fact that it is a newspaper. (*Ser tp* in the 008 field has the value *n* for newspaper.)

The note for the source of the title proper (12.7B3) is combined with the note citing the item on which the description is based (12.7B23).

Leader   nas   a
Fixed Data 008
  Entrd: nnnnnn Pub st: c Dates: 19uu-9999 Ctry: cau
  Frequn: w   Regulr: r ISDS: Ser tp: p
  Form of orig item: Form of item: Nature of work:
  Nature of cont: Govt pub: Conf pub: 0 Titl pag: u
  Indx: u Cum ind: u Alphabt: a S/L ent: 0 Lang: eng
  Mod rec: Source: d

032   906620 $b USPS

130 00 Valley Press (Felton, Calif.)

245 00 Valley Press.

260 00 Felton, CA : $b [s.n.,

300   v. : $b ill. ; $c 48 cm.

310   Weekly each Wednesday

520   A newspaper for the San Lorenzo Valley, Calif.

500   Description based on: Vol. 30, no. 27 (June 6, 1990);
       caption title.

REVIEW QUESTIONS

1. Which rules tell how to choose the chief source of information for an item?

2. For the title *Dr. Burgess's Atlas of Marine Aquarium Fishes,* by Dr. Warren E. Burgess III, which rule tells whether or not to transcribe *Dr. Burgess's* as part of the title? Which rule tells whether to transcribe *Dr.* and *III* in the statement of responsibility?

3. Which rule tells whether one must record the duration or playing time of an item such as a sound recording or videorecording?

4. Which rule tells how to describe items made up of two or more components which belong to distinct material types, such as a set of slides and a sound cassette?

5. Rule 0.24 says to describe a printed monograph in microform as a microform, using the rules in Chapter 11. Rule 1.11A says to describe a facsimile, photocopy or other reproduction of printed material by giving the data relating to the facsimile, etc., in all areas except the note area. The original version is described in the note area. Should you follow these rules?

6. How does LC now describe works with pagination like the examples in Rules 2.5B7 and 2.5B8? Where is this information available?

7. Which rules tell what chapter to use to describe a globe?

8. Which *AACR2R* rule tells you which MARC format to use when you create a machine-readable cataloging record for that globe?

9. Which chapter of *AACR2R* is used to catalog an atlas of maps?

10. Which USMARC specification is defined for inputting the cataloging record for that atlas?

11. Which rule tells how to record a title for a collection of ledger sheets from a nineteenth-century Monterey fish cannery?

12. Which rule should you use to describe a book with the title: *The New York Times Great Songs of the 70s: 81 Songs for Voice, Piano and Guitar*?

13. Which rule gives the instructions for the physical description of an audio recording on compact disc or cassette tape?

14. What part of the rule tells whether to give the playing speed for these?

15. Which part of the rule tells whether to give the size for these?

16. Which rule tells how to record a title for a videorecording of a college commencement ceremony made by a member of the audience? (There are no title frames or accompanying printed information.)

17. Which rules tell how to record place, publisher and date for such a videorecording?

18. You must catalog a collection of posters issued for the Monterey Jazz Festivals. Which chapter should you use?

19. What is a notable difference between Rule 7.0B1 and 9.0B1?

20. Which rule tells whether to record the source of the title proper when cataloging computer files? What is the difference between that rule and parallel rules in chapters for other materials?

21. List the chapters to use for describing each of the following items: (1) a relief map; (2) a model of your new library building; (3) an IBM personal computer; (4) a computer program; (5) slides of paintings by Degas; (6) a bust of Beethoven; (7) a facsimile reprint of the Declaration of Independence; (8) a military survival kit in a labeled box; (9) a microscope slide with a fruit-fly specimen; (10) a computer game; (11) a library catalog published for the first time on microfiche.

22. If the title proper of a serial changes, you must make separate records for each title. Which rule tells what constitutes a change in title proper?

23. Which rule tells how to choose the main entry for a sound recording of Shakespeare's *Hamlet* with Lawrence Olivier reading the lead role? What would the main entry be?

24. Which rule tells how to choose the main entry for a videorecording of a production of *Hamlet* with Olivier in the lead role? What would the main entry be?

25. Is there a special rule for choice of main entry that might apply to music videos?

26. Are there any examples in Chapter 21, "Choice of Access Points," for a motion picture or videorecording?

27. You have a work which appears to be a collaboration between an artist and a writer. Which rule tells how to choose the main entry for this work? You have an edition of another work, *Alice in Wonderland,* which has been illustrated by Arthur Rackham. Which rule tells you how to choose the main entry for this work?

28. What is the first step for a cataloger in determining the established form for any name or uniform title?

29. The contemporary novelist Joyce Carol Oates publishes under two pseudonyms as well as her real name. Which rule governs the form of her name that you select for cataloging her works?

30. Which rule tells how to construct the headings for Monterey County and the city of Monterey?

31. Which rule tells whether or not to abbreviate the word "County" in the heading?

32. Do the rules give any special instructions on how to construct a heading for a military installation or an airport?

33. Which rule tells how to enter a corporate body?

34. Which rule gives the definition of a corporate body?

35. Which rule tells you what additions to make to the name of a local church?

36. Which rule lists the types of government agencies that are entered subordinately?

37. Does the name *Santa Cruz County Sanitation District* fall into any of those categories?

38. Which chapter tells how to construct uniform titles?

39. Some uniform titles are tagged as 130s, others as 240s. What is the difference between them?

40. Is there a special rule for distinguishing different serial publications that have identical titles proper?

41. Which rule tells how to construct the uniform title for a libretto of Aida?

42. Which rule tells what elements to include in the uniform title for a piece of music whose title consists solely of a type of composition?

43. Which rules tell how to construct the uniform title heading for a King James version of the New Testament published in 1960?

44. You are cataloging a Spanish language book that has the statement "3a. edicion" in it. In the bibliographic utility to which you are contributing, you find a record that matches this work, except for the edition statement which reads "2a. edicion." Where should you look to find out whether you need to input a new record?

45. You want to know how the Library of Congress applies a particular rule in AACR2R. In what publication can you look for that information?

46. You don't read Chinese but must make an original cataloging record for a work entirely in Chinese. A staff member who reads Chinese but doesn't do original cataloging is going to help you. In what tool will your assistant find the romanization table for converting Chinese characters?

ANSWERS TO REVIEW QUESTIONS

1. Which rules tell how to choose the chief source of information for an item?

    The general rule is 1.0A. See 2.0B for books, 3.0B for cartographic materials, 4.0B for manuscripts, and so forth.

2. For the title *Dr. Burgess's Atlas of Marine Aquarium Fishes,* by Dr. Warren E. Burgess III, which rule tells whether or not to transcribe *Dr. Burgess's* as part of the title? Which rule tells whether to transcribe *Dr.* and *III* in the statement of responsibility?

    1.1B2, and 1.1F7.

3. Which rule tells whether one must record the duration or playing time of an item such as a sound recording or videorecording?

    1.5B4. (See also "duration" in the index to *AACR2R.*)

4. Which rule tells how to describe items made up of two or more components which belong to distinct material types, such as a set of slides and a sound cassette?

    1.10, "Items Made up of Several Types of Material."

5. Rule 0.24 says to describe a printed monograph in microform as a microform, using the rules in Chapter 11. Rule 1.11A says to describe a facsimile, photocopy or other reproduction of printed material by giving the data relating to the facsimile, etc., in all areas except the note area. The original version is described in the note area. Should you follow these rules?

    For published facsimile reprints and original microform publications, you should follow rule 1.11 and rules in other chapters, as appropriate. However, catalogers following LC practice should do the opposite for certain materials (*LCRI* 1.11): for microform and "on demand" photocopy reproductions of previously existing materials, describe the *original* in all areas except the note area, then describe the reproduction in the note area.

6. How does LC now describe works with pagination like the examples in Rules 2.5B7 and 2.5B8? Where is this information available?

   In its LCRIs, published in *Cataloging Service bulletin* #44 (spring 1989), LC says to record as follows:
   2.5B7:   1 v. (unpaged)
   2.5B8:   1 v. (various pagings)

7. Which rules tell what chapter to use to describe a globe?

   3.0A and 10.0A.

8. Which *AACR2R* rule tells you which MARC format to use when you create a machine-readable cataloging record for that globe?

   None. You must consult the documentation for the bibliographic utility or data base you are using. (USMARC defines the Maps specification for globes.)

9. Which chapter of AACR2R *is used to catalog an atlas of maps?*

   Chapter 3, "Cartographic Materials."

10. Which USMARC specification is defined for inputting the cataloging record for that atlas?

   The Maps specification. (In OCLC, though, the atlas record is input in the OCLC Books Format.)

11. Which rule tells how to record a title for a collection of ledger sheets from a nineteenth-century Monterey fish cannery?

   4.1B2, p. 126.

12. Which rule should you use to describe a book with the title: The New York Times Great Songs of the 70s: 81 Songs for Voice, Piano and Guitar?

   Chapter 5, "Music."

13. Which rule gives the instructions for the physical description of an audio recording on compact disc or cassette tape?

   6.5.

14. What part of the rule tells whether to give the playing speed for these?

> **6.5C3. Do not give playing speed if it is standard for the item.**

15. Which part of the rule tells whether to give the size for these?

> **6.5D5. Give the dimensions if other than the standard.**

16. Which rule tells how to record a title for a videorecording of a college commencement ceremony made by a member of the audience? (There are no title frames or accompanying printed information.)

> **7.1B2, 1.1B7.**

17. Which rules tell how to record place, publisher and date for such a videorecording?

> **7.4C2, 7.4D2, 7.4F3.**

18. You must catalog a collection of posters issued for the Monterey Jazz Festivals. Which chapter should you use?

> **Chapter 8, "Graphic Materials."**

19. What is a notable difference between Rule 7.0B1 and 9.0B1?

> **In cataloging motion pictures and videorecordings, the cataloger is expected to view the title frames (7.0B1). For the cataloging of computer files, though, *AACR2R* specifically says that the cataloger without access to equipment to read the files may describe the item from information that is available (9.0B1 and first footnote on p. 222.)**

20. Which rule tells whether to record the source of the title proper when cataloging computer files? What is the difference between that rule and parallel rules in chapters for other materials?

> **9.7B3 says "always" give the source of the title proper when cataloging computer files. The source of the title proper for other materials is given only under certain conditions prescribed in the chapters for those materials.**

21. List the chapters to use for describing each of the following items: (1) a relief map; (2) a model of your new library

building; (3) an IBM personal computer; (4) a computer program; (5) slides of paintings by Degas; (6) a bust of Beethoven; (7) a facsimile reprint of the Declaration of Independence; (8) a military survival kit in a labeled box; (9) a microscope slide with a fruit-fly specimen; (10) a computer game; (11) a library catalog published for the first time on microfiche.

(1) **Chapter 3**   (5) **Chapter 8**   (9) **Chapter 10**
(2) **Chapter 10**   (6) **Chapter 10**   (10) **Chapter 9**
(3) **Chapter 10**   (7) **Chapter 2**   (11) **Chapter 11**
(4) **Chapter 8**   (8) **Chapter 1**

22. If the title proper of a serial changes, you must make separate records for each title. Which rule tells what constitutes a change in title proper?

    21.2A1.

23. Which rule tells how to choose the main entry for a sound recording of Shakespeare's Hamlet *with Lawrence Olivier reading the lead role? What would the main entry be?*

    21.23A1. Shakespeare, William, 1564-1616.

24. Which rule tells how to choose the main entry for a videorecording of a production of Hamlet *with Olivier in the lead role? What would the main entry be?*

    21.9, then 21.6C2. Main entry under title.

25. Is there a special rule for choice of main entry that might apply to music videos?

    Yes. Rule 21.1B2e.

26. Are there any examples in Chapter 21, "Choice of Access Points," for a motion picture or videorecording?

    Yes, there's one: the next-to-last example on p. 319. It illustrates Rule 21.1B2e.

27. You have a work which appears to be a collaboration between an artist and a writer. Which rule tells how to choose the main entry for this work? You have an edition of another work, Alice in Wonderland, *which has been illustrated by Arthur Rackham. Which rule tells you how to choose the main entry for this work?*

Rule 21.24 covers the first work. Rule 21.11A1 applies to the second work.

28. What is the first step for a cataloger in determining the established form for any name or uniform title?

    Search the Library of Congress Name Authority File. (If the authorized form is not found, it must be established according to *AACR2R* Chapters 22-25.)

29. The contemporary novelist Joyce Carol Oates publishes under two pseudonyms as well as her real name. Which rule governs the form of her name that you select for cataloging her works?

    22.2B3.

30. Which rule tells how to construct the headings for Monterey County and the city of Monterey?

    23.2A1 and 23.4C2.

31. Which rule tells whether or not to abbreviate the word "County" in the heading?

    Appendix B.14A.

32. Do the rules give any special instructions on how to construct a heading for a military installation or an airport?

    **No, but the LC rule interpretation for 23.1 does, e.g.,
    March Air Force Base (Calif.)
    San Francisco International Airport (Calif.)**

33. Which rule tells how to enter a corporate body?

    24.1.

34. Which rule gives the definition of a corporate body?

    21.1B1.

35. Which rule tells you what additions to make to the name of a local church?

    24.10 A & B.

36. Which rule lists the types of government agencies that are entered subordinately?

24.18.

37. Does the name Santa Cruz County Sanitation District *fall into any of those categories?*

   No. (Use 24.17).

38. Which chapter tells how to construct uniform titles?

   Chapter 25.

39. Some uniform titles are tagged as 130s, others as 240s. What is the difference between them?

   Tag *130* is for a uniform title used as a main entry heading; tag *240* is for a uniform title that follows a main entry heading (100, 110, or 111).

40. Is there a special rule for distinguishing different serial publications that have identical titles proper?

   No, but 25.2A(3) has a provision that suggests constructing uniform title headings to distinguish different works with identical titles proper. Rule 25.5B, "Conflict Resolution," tells generally how to construct such uniform title headings. LC has an extensive rule interpretation for 25.5B explaining how to construct such headings for serials.

41. Which rule tells how to construct the uniform title for a libretto of Aida?

   25.35E.

42. Which rule tells what elements to include in the uniform title for a piece of music whose title consists solely of a type of composition?

   25.30C.

43. Which rules tell how to construct the uniform title heading for a King James version of the New Testament published in 1960?

   25.17A; 25.18A1, 2, 10, 11, 13.

44. You are cataloging a Spanish language book that has the statement "3a. edicion" in it. In the bibliographic utility to which you are contributing, you find a record that matches this

work, except for the edition statement which reads "2a. edicion." Where should you look to find out whether you need to input a new record?

Consult the input standards for your bibliographic utility. OCLC, for example, does not treat romance language publications with such edition statements as new editions that justify inputting a new record. (The first LCRI for rule 1.0 discusses the matter of edition versus copy.)

45. You want to know how the Library of Congress applies a particular rule in AACR2R. In what publication can you look for that information?

The Library of Congress *Cataloging Service bulletin* contains this information. These interpretations are also published in a cumulative edition with periodic updates.

46. You don't read Chinese but must make an original cataloging record for a work entirely in Chinese. A staff member who reads Chinese but doesn't do original cataloging is going to help you. In what tool will your assistant find the romanization table for converting Chinese characters?

The Library of Congress *Cataloging Service bulletin* #118 (summer 1976).

BIBLIOGRAPHY

BASIC SOURCES

Anglo-American Cataloguing Rules. 2nd ed., 1988 revision. Edited by Michael Gorman and Paul W. Winkler. Ottawa: Canadian Library Association; Chicago: American Library Association, 1988.

> The current cataloging code, *AACR2R.*

Library of Congress Rule Interpretations. 2nd ed. Washington, D.C.: Cataloging Distribution Service, Library of Congress, 1989.

> A cumulation of currently valid LC rule interpretations of *AACR2R.* Updated periodically. The LCRIs are also published in the Library of Congress *Cataloging Service Bulletin,* each issue of which also contains a cumulative index to the LCRIs arranged by rule number.

Name Authorities Cumulative Microform Edition. Washington, D.C.: Library of Congress.

> Includes LC forms for personal and corporate names, conference headings, uniform titles, and series established according to *AACR2R.* Also contains forms for geographic names of political and civil jurisdictions. Issued quarterly; each issue is fully cumulative.

> The LC name authority records are available in several versions. In addition to the microform edition, a CD-ROM version is distributed by the Library of Congress. Magnetic tape versions have been loaded by bibliographic utilities for online availability. These tapes are also processed by vendors and networks for application in local online public access catalogs.

USMARC Concise Format for Bibliographic, Authority, and Holdings Data. Prepared by Network Development and MARC Standards Office. Washington: Cataloging Distribution Service, Library of Congress, 1988.

> An inexpensive, single-volume work that provides a *concise* description of USMARC. Describes each field, each character position of the fixed-length data element fields, and the indicators in the variable data fields. The full text of USMARC is published as *USMARC Format for Bibliographic Data Including Guidelines for Content Designation.* Both the full document and the concise version are kept up-to-date by the periodic issuing of new and replacement pages.

> In order to describe an item and enter it into a computerized system, a cataloging agency will need to consult the documentation of the cataloging utility or system to which records are contributed. This documentation will include manuals for tagging and coding records in USMARC-based formats.

AUXILIARY SOURCES

The following interpretive manuals may be useful to catalogers who wish further information on various materials.

Maxwell, Margaret F. *Handbook for AACR2 1988 Revision: Explaining and Illustrating the Anglo-American Cataloguing Rules.* Chicago, London: American Library Association, 1989.

> A comprehensive work on the current cataloging code. Includes cataloging examples and references to the rule interpretations of the Library of Congress.

Hensen, Steven L. *Archives, Personal Papers, and Manuscripts: a Cataloging Manual for Archival Repositories, Historical Societies, and Manuscript Libraries.* 2nd ed. Chicago: Society of American Archivists, 1989.

> The standard manual for augmenting *AACR2R* in the cataloging of archival and manuscript materials.

Olson Nancy B. *Cataloging Microcomputer Software: A Manual to Accompany AACR 2 Chapter 9, Computer Files.* Englewood, Colo.: Libraries Unlimited, 1988.

> Contains a history and annotated bibliography on the cataloging of software, as well as 100 examples of catalog records for computer materials.

Cartographic Materials: A Manual of Interpretation for AACR2. Prepared by the Anglo-American Cataloguing Committee for Cartographic Materials. Chicago: American Library Association, 1982.

> Deals with the technical vocabulary and other problems related to the descriptive cataloging of cartographic materials.

Rogers, JoAnn V. and Jerry D. Saye. *Nonprint Cataloging for Multimedia Collections: a Guide Based on AACR2.* 2nd ed. Littleton, Colo.: Libraries Unlimited, 1987.

> Contains cataloging examples for a wide range of nonbook materials.

Betz, Elisabeth W. *Graphic Materials: Rules for Describing Original Items and Historical Collections.* Washington, D.C.: Library of Congress, 1982.

> Provides guidance for cataloging graphic materials within the general structure and theory of *AACR2.*

Frost, Carolyn O. *Media Access and Organization: A Cataloging and Reference Sources Guide for Nonbook Materials.* Englewood, Colo.: Libraries Unlimited, 1989.

> Analyzes problem areas in the description of every type of nonbook material. Attention is also given to subject access. Cataloging examples are provided, as well as listings of reference tools which assist in the cataloging process.

Leong, Carol L.H. *Serials Cataloging Handbook: An Illustrative Guide to the Use of AACR2 and LC Rule Interpretations.* Chicago: American Library Association, 1989.

> A comprehensive work, with analysis of rules, and attention to numerous serials problems. Contains 178 cataloging examples and USMARC tagging information as represented in the *OCLC Serials Format.*

CONSER Editing Guide. Prepared by staff of the Serial Record Division under the direction of the CONSER Operations Coordinator. Washington, D.C.: Serial Record Division, Library of Congress, 1986.

> Provides detailed instructions conforming to *AACR2R,* the CONSER Project, and USMARC. Examples illustrate correct cataloging and input conventions. Kept up-to-date by the periodic issuing of new and replacement pages.

Hallam, Adele. *Cataloging Rules for the Description of Looseleaf Publications.* Washington, D.C.: Office for Descriptive Cataloging, Library of Congress, 1989.

A tool for solving descriptive cataloging problems related to publications which are issued in looseleaf format for updating.

Cataloging Government Documents: a Manual of Interpretation for AACR2. Bernadine Abbott Hoduski, editor. Chicago: American Library Association, 1984.

Rules especially pertinent to the cataloging of government documents are discussed. Cataloging examples are provided. No new rules or additions to AACR2 are proposed.

Saye, Jerry D. and Sherry L. Vellucci. *Notes in the Catalog Record: Based on AACR2 and LC Rule Interpretations*. Chicago: American Library Association, 1989.

Provides guidance and examples in the formulation of notes for descriptive cataloging.

Thomas, Nancy G. and Rosanna O'Neil. *Notes for Serials Cataloging*. Littleton, Colo.: Libraries Unlimited, 1986.

Provides sample notes for serials cataloging, arranged by USMARC tag.

APPENDIX

This section contains copies of additional blank workforms in the USMARC specifications.

BOOKS WORKFORM

Leader   nam   a
Fixed Data 008
  Entrd: nnnnnn Dat tp: Dates: Ctry: Illus:
  Int lvl: Repr: Cont: Govt pub: Conf pub: Festsch:
  Indx: M/E: Fict: Bio: Lang: Mod rec: Source:

020

041 _

1_ _ _

245 _ _

250

260 _

300

4_ _ _

5_

7_ _ _

7_ _ _

8_ _ _

ARCHIVAL AND MANUSCRIPTS CONTROL WORKFORM

Leader   nbm   a
Fixed Data 008
  Entrd: nnnnnn Dat tp: Dates: ,   Ctry:
  Form of item: Lang: Mod rec: Source:

1__ _

245 _ _

260

300

5__

5__

5__

7__ _ _

COMPUTER FILES WORKFORM

Leader   nmm   a

Fixed Data 008

  Entrd: nnnnnn   Dat tp: Dates: ,   Ctry: Frequn:

  Regulr: Type of File: Govt Pub:

  Lang: Mod rec: Source:

1__ _

245 _ _

260

300

538

5__

5__

5__

5__

7__ _ _

7__ _ _

7__ _ _

MAPS WORKFORM

Leader   nem   a
Fixed Data 008
 Entrd: nnnnnn Dat tp: Dates: ,   Ctry: Relief:
 Project: Prime merid: MatType: Govt Pub:
 Indx: Form: Lang: Mod rec   Source:

034 _

1__ _

245 _ _

255

260 _

300

5__

5__

7__ _ _

7__ _ _

MUSIC WORKFORM

Leader   ncm   a
Fixed Data 008
 Entrd: nnnnnn Dat tp: Dates: Ctry: Comp:
 Format: Audience: Form of item: Accomp mat:
 LitText: M/E: Lang: Mod rec: Source:

007

020

028 _ _

047

041 _

1_ _ _ _

245 _ _

260 _

300

4_ _ _ _

5_ _

5_ _

7_ _ _ _

7_ _ _ _

8_ _ _ _

SOUND RECORDING WORKFORM

Leader   njm   a
Fixed Data 008
  Entrd: nnnnnn   Dat tp: Dates: Ctry: Comp:
  Format: Audience: Form of item: Accomp mat:
  LitText: M/E: Lang: Mod rec: Source:

007

020

028 _ _

047

041 _

1_ _ _ _

245 _ _

260 _

300

4_ _ _ _

5_ _

5_ _

7_ _ _ _

7_ _ _ _

8_ _ _ _

VISUAL MATERIALS WORKFORM

Leader   n_m   a
Fixed Data 008
  Entrd: nnnnnn   Dat tp: Dates: ,   Ctry: Leng:
  Audi: Accomp mat: Govt pub: MEBE: Type mat:
  Tech: Lang: Mod rec: Source:

007

1__ _

245 _ _

260

300

5__

5__

5__

7__ __

SERIAL WORKFORM

Leader   nas   a_
Fixed Data 008
  Entrd: nnnnnn Pub st: Dates: -   Ctry:
  Frequn: Regulr: ISDS: Ser tp:
  Form of orig item: Form of item: Nature of work:
  Nature of cont: Govt pub: Conf pub: Titl pag:
  Indx: Cum ind: Alphabt: S/L ent: Lang:
  Mod rec: Source:

1__ _ _

245 _ _

246 _ _

260 0 0

300

310

362 _

5__

5__

7__ __

7__ __

Larry Millsap is Head, Bibliographic Records Section, and Acting Head, Reference Services Section, University of California, Santa Cruz.

Terry Ellen Ferl is Principal Cataloger, University of California, Santa Cruz.

Book design: Gloria Brown
Cover design: Gregory Apicella
Typography: Roberts/Churcher